# Keep Going!

# Keep Going!

## A user-friendly guide to the Christian life and missions

Rodney Hui

LONDON ● COLORADO SPRINGS ● HYDERABAD

13  12  11  10  09  08  07    9  8  7  6  5  4  3

Reprinted 2004, 2007
First published in 2004 by Authentic Media
9 Holdom Avenue, Bletchley, Milton Keynes, Bucks., MK1 1UQ, UK
1820 Jet Stream Drive, Colorado Springs, CO 80921, USA
OM Authentic Media, Medchal Road, Jeedimetla Village,
Secunderabad 500 055, A.P., India
www.authenticmedia.co.uk
Authentic Media is a division of IBS-STL U.K., limited by
guarantee, with its Registered Office at Kingstown Broadway,
Carlisle, Cumbria CA3 0HA.  Registered in England & Wales No.
1216232. Registered charity 270162

**British Library Cataloguing in Publication Data**

A catalogue record for this book is available from the
British Library


ISBN-13 978-1-85078-562-0


Cover design by Phil Houghton
Print Management by Adare Carwin
Printed in Great Britain by J.H. Haynes and Co., Sparkford

# Contents

**Part Three – *Gone!***

# Commendations

Interesting, honest, vision building, encouraging . . . I have known Rodney for over 30 years and he has the walk that goes with the talk, so please hear what he has to say in this dynamic, cutting-edge book. It will help keep you in the race.

*George Verwer,*
*Founder, Operation Mobilisation*

He came to the house where we were living in Changi, Singapore early one Sunday morning . . . Rodney Hui was young – and eager to grow, to learn and to serve God. That eagerness and enthusiasm has continued unabated over the years. As we have worked together in the Ships Ministry and in the East Asia/Pacific region, I have observed his commitment to the principles he outlines in this book.

The examples Rodney describes are people I admire, most of whom I know well. Their dedication and commitment are authentic. He shares truth out of real life experience, demonstrated by real people, gathered from a wealth of experience and supported by a commitment to practice.

This book deserves not only a focused reading but also faithful application to one's own life.

**Allan Adams, former Ship's Director of Logos and Doulos and pioneer of OM East Asia**

Having given the biblical basis, how-to's and details of DIY, Rodney engages the reader further with adventure-filled stories that touch the heart, challenge the mind and move the feet.

**Dr Wei-Leong Goh, Founder, Linking Hands and Chairman, OM Singapore Board**

Rodney Hui begins with a beautiful story which does not have a perfect ending. So the book tells many such stories – of simple joys and hard struggles – from Caribbean reggae and Japanese bath to Cambodian children and soap-making in Nepal. He expounds missions at the ground level, sometimes heart-breaking, sometimes heart-warming, but always calling us to run with the dream that one day will surely be fulfilled: every nation of earth calling Jesus Lord.

**David Wong, Vice President, International Training, Haggai Institute**

More impressed with God's greatness than with the challenge, Rodney has in an inspired, very practical and humorous way, laid out a road map for us to bring Him glory.

For some this road map will show the way. For others the map will bring them back on course, while for yet others it will serve as a reminder of what God has done.

Keep going – it's worth it!

**Francois Vosloo, Operation Mobilisation**

# Foreword

*Been There, Done That*, Rodney's first book, has been enjoyed by many people I've spoken to. Some people have experienced significant life revolution through reading it and are now in a different part of the world serving God. Part Two – *Keep Going!*, is an excellent addition. Twenty eight years in missions gives Rodney a strong platform from which to write. Here you will find excellent practical tips to living the Christian life, a basic introduction to missions and exciting, stimulating examples from those who've heard the call of God and responded in obedience.

I believe this book may well have an even greater impact than Rodney's first, so don't read it unless you're prepared to hear from God, with all the practical consequences of that.

You'll find the read enjoyable, informative and challenging. As a fellow runner, I particularly appreciated the last chapter!

*Peter Maiden*
*International Director of*
*Operation Mobilisation*

# Introduction

The response to my first book *Been There, Done That* has been most encouraging. One lady wrote to me to say that she is now serving in Myanmar all because she read it. This alone brings me great satisfaction. Former OMers and present OM workers shared that they could identify with the book – like I was writing about them. Readers have been very kind in their comments. I have yet to receive my first brickbat!

While *Been There, Done That* is autobiographical, *Keep Going!* is like a treatise. After twenty-eight years in the missions scene, I reckon I am somewhat qualified to write on this subject. I want it to be a user-friendly guide for the ordinary Christian in discovering missions. Admittedly this is not a first on this subject, but coming from an Asian, perhaps it will give a different slant to it. My good friend, Dr Rajendran, general secretary of the India Missions Association, lamented to me that Asians are not very good in documenting that which we know and experience. We are the poorer for it. This book is my feeble attempt at addressing this shortage. It is not meant to be a scholarly work. If anything, it is written in the only way I know – simply and down to earth. Please accept my apologies if you are expecting a better piece of work.

I have divided this book into three parts. *Part One – Keep believing* talks about a journey in faith. It begins with a story and continues to give practical tips on survival as a Christian. They are not formulas where success is guaranteed, but tips that will get you on the right track. Obviously the chapter I enjoyed most is Chapter Two – Jesus, the Person who is the reason behind all that I am and do.

*Part Two – Going, going . . .* introduces readers to missions, as I see it. This section contains my thoughts, my talks and my passion of the past twenty-eight years. In the course of writing, I discovered the greatest ease in expression. When you have been breathing nothing but missions all these years, it should not come as a surprise. Indeed, God had taken me through the mill, and my hope in this section is to get you going in missions.

*Part Three – Gone!* contains stories of people I know and admire. Having told my own story in my first book, I thought I should write about people whom I have the privilege of working with. I trust the stories of these ordinary people are an inspiration to you. I end that section with some light reading on my more recent travels.

I conclude this book with a brief epilogue about my favourite pastime - running. The Christian life and missions, after all, is for the long run – i.e. for life!

*Rodney Hui*
*68, Lorong 16, Geylang*
*#03-06 Association Building*
*Singapore 398889*
*Email: rodhui@pacific.net.sg*

# PART ONE

*Keep believing*

# Chapter One

# First thing first

'. . . my peace I give you. I do not give to you as the world gives . . .' – Jesus

(Jn. 14:27, NIV)

It came unexpectedly.

Irene my wife, Justin and Marianne, my son and daughter, were at home when Lawrence phoned to invite us out to dinner. It had been a while since we had a meal with Lawrence. He was bringing Sally, his wife, and their son, Eugene.

After a fabulous seafood meal, we invited them to our flat for a cuppa. The TV was left on – an Asian habit even in the presence of guests. It is treated as part of the family! After about an hour of small talk with frequent glances at the TV, Lawrence and family were ready to take their leave.

'By the way, Chong,' Lawrence said, calling me by my Chinese name, 'before we leave, I have a question to ask you.'

'What is it?' I asked.

With some hesitation, he asked, 'How do I become a Christian?'

My heart missed a few beats. I saw Irene turn her head away from the TV to look at Lawrence. Justin, at eight years of age then, had an expression on his face that spoke of surprise. Surprise was probably an understatement, under the circumstances.

Lawrence is tall for a Chinese. Burly. With the added weight and size, he is someone you wouldn't mind having on your side in a threatening situation. For as long as I have known him, he had always been a devout, superstitious believer of Chinese religions.

My memory flashed back to a night in September in 1975 when I first shared with him the gospel – the good news of Jesus Christ. I sensed the urgency just before I left on the MV Logos to go to India and westward. Not knowing how long I would be gone, I grabbed the only opportunity. I could still remember his response – 'I'm not sure.' Not wanting to be pushy, I left it at that.

In the next twenty-one years, I followed Lawrence's religious pursuits with dismay. On one visit to his previous home, I counted no less than 32 idols of various deities sitting on altars in a room dedicated to them. I did not give up praying for Lawrence's salvation. My family would pray for him and his family. It was a great encouragement when his son Eugene turned to the Lord. But to be honest, we were not very hopeful with Lawrence. We figured it would take nothing less than a miracle to see Lawrence come to faith in Jesus Christ.

Then he moved house. As soon as I entered his new home, the first thing I saw was a three foot tall golden statue sitting on top of the main altar. This was in the place of the multiple deities he had once had. This particular statue was that of his spiritual godfather, Lawrence admitted. He was a renowned and revered monk then living outside of Bangkok. Lawrence would make regular pilgrimages to his 'godfather'. He spared no expense on this relationship, pouring thousands of dollars in donations into the temple in Bangkok. The frequency of his trips increased as the months went by, to a point where the strain was beginning to show in his marriage. Sally, his wife, began to wonder if he was keeping a mistress in Bangkok, when all along he was really trying to fill an emptiness in his heart.

With this background, you would understand my surprise when Lawrence popped the unexpected question. None of us suspected that this was coming. But before I got over-excited and lost my equilibrium, I asked him the obvious question.

'Why do you want to become a Christian?'

This was when he started pouring out his woes.

For all the years of dedication and genuine search, he had neither found nor felt peace in his heart. He went after idols, patronised temples, worshipped various deities and even adopted a monk who was now dead, only to arrive at a dead end. Life was empty and he had no answers. He could not fill that void. The dissatisfaction and unsettledness persisted.

He recounted how, several years earlier, he had envied his mother-in-law who had died peacefully in her sleep. She was an illiterate woman from the countryside outside the Malaysian town of Batu Pahat who had come to know and love Jesus Christ several years before her death.

'She was poor by normal standards, and did not read or write,' Lawrence said, 'but she died the most peaceful death.' His mother-in-law had felt unwell in church one Sunday. On returning to her attap house, she showered, changed into fresh clothes, went to lie down on her bed, and entered into the Lord's presence. Just like that!

'This is the kind of peace I want, and don't have,' Lawrence finally confessed. All these years it had eluded him. And he was determined that he would find it that night. Of all the Christians he knew, he wanted to hear it from me, he said.

'What about Sally?' I asked. I didn't want his wife to miss out on this opportunity. In the Asian culture, the head of the family is often the key to the salvation of the entire family.

'I am waiting for him,' was Sally's measured response. She had been prepared for some time already but she wanted to wait for the head of the house to lead the way.

It was my delight that night to lead both of them to faith in Jesus Christ. It was special in that God had answered after more than twenty-one years of prayer. But what made it especially thrilling was that Lawrence is one of my brothers and Sally, my sister-in-law.

The story did not end there. Now that he had pledged allegiance to Jesus, he wanted to know how to deal with his idolatrous past; specifically, he wanted to know what to do with the idols in his home. He wanted to cut the bonds that bound him to the control of the deities. That night, I suggested several things for him to do. He was determined to make a clean break.

The problems started soon after that. Lawrence began to have nightmares. He began to behave strangely in the day, as if in a daze. Sally was getting worried that Lawrence was not himself. Thankfully, they were not left alone. A close friend who is a committed Christian got her Mandarin-speaking church involved. A small group, led by the pastor, made follow-up visits. They prayed for and studied the Bible with them. Still the nightmares persisted.

It is not uncommon for a person who had practised idolatry, having turned to Christ, to experience spiritual opposition. When Christ comes into a person's life, the

Holy Spirit begins to indwell the person, taking residence in the person's being. Obviously, previous (evil) spirits that the person had made room for will not give up their domain that easily. This was true with Lawrence. Evil spirits were entrenched in areas of his life. Breaking free from them would involve a clash of spiritual powers. The outcome, however, is obvious for the Christian, for he that is in us is greater than he that is in the world (see 1 Jn. 4:4).We are taught that Jesus, in dying on the cross, totally and completely defeated the enemy, the devil and all his hosts.

Lawrence informed me that he would be woken up in the middle of the night. A monk, then another, would appear before him.

'I was not afraid of the monks,' he admitted. He would tell the spirits that he was now following Jesus and no longer sought to follow them, and that they should leave him alone. The spirits left him. But what Lawrence was terrified of was the apparition in a long white robe with locks of long hair. And he was losing sleep and not a little sanity. In response, I gave him some tapes of Chinese Christian hymns and choruses to listen to.

'Next time, when this happens, play the cassettes,' I instructed him. Evil spirits hate the worship of the Lord Jesus. Worship songs only reminded the spirits of their defeat and the victory in Christ. Secondly, I encouraged him to read the Bible. This is because the word of God would strengthen his faith and transform his mind. As a new Christian, Lawrence needed to grow in his new found faith. Prayer was an important part of growth.

This worked. Several weeks later, it was a much better Lawrence who phoned me to say that the evil spirits no longer bothered him. Lawrence and his wife also became active members of a Chinese Presbyterian church.

The following year, my family attended their baptism. Later, they became members of the church choir. Of late, Lawrence is thinking about missions.

Well, what is the moral of the story? I can think of several. Persevering in prayer is one. God does not forget even if we have forgotten to pray. God's sovereignty in the lives of people is another. Presbyterians, like me, will appreciate this point! Three, God's timing is perfect. Four, he uses the testimonies of his children – remember the illiterate but God-loving and simple mother-in-law?

The lesson I want to highlight is that if you genuinely search for peace, you will find it. You will not find it through human means, through some sort of learned meditation or yoga (or some New Age spirituality in disguise), through attending a course that teaches a pet formula, or through joining a peaceful cause. Do not believe it when peace is promised to you at no expense, or in anything or anyone save Jesus Christ. If you do, you will be disillusioned. True peace can only come from the Author of peace, the Prince of Peace himself, Jesus Christ.

So, how does one become a Christian?

It is simple. The Bible says 'Believe in the Lord Jesus, and you will be saved' (Acts 16:31, NIV). Jesus is central to being a Christian. Not self, not church and not some other personality.

When you believe in someone, you do and follow what the person says. This is the hard part of being a Christian. It takes a lifetime of obedience to do that. But the first step is meant to be simple. Once you have Jesus, you can start afresh and anew in life. The following chapters will help you start right, but you need to sort out this important issue in your life first.

*(Postscript – With missions on their hearts, Lawrence and Sally did get to Kazakstan in the hope of setting up a petroleum*

business. *They suffered a major setback when, on the third day, Lawrence slipped on ice and fell. Sally fractured her arm in another fall. Lawrence was airlifted home. After emergency surgery, he is presently undergoing intensive physiotherapy to regain mobility of his body and limbs. Progress has been slow.)*

# Chapter Two

# Jesus

It was my first time in Jordan. Kamal, my Sudanese friend and colleague had offered to host the executive meetings of OM in the capital, Amman. I always look forward to visiting a country I have not been to before.

'It was in Jordan that the Trinity met on earth!' I never saw it that way until Issam, a Jordanian friend, proudly announced it. I was all the more pleased to be there! How could I ever forget the voice from heaven saying, 'This is my Son, whom I love; with him I am well pleased' (Mt. 3:17, NIV) spoken two thousand years ago by the River Jordan. From this verbal affirmation of the Father to his Son, we catch a glimpse of the perfect love and relationship between the heavenly Father and his beloved Son.

For several days, we stayed at a Catholic retreat centre located just outside Amman. The environment was peaceful and quiet, with the silence broken only by the chirping of the birds and bleating of the sheep. The early morning was particularly contemplative. The Catholic nuns had created a garden with icons and symbols leading contemplators to ponder on the suffering of Jesus. That contemplation eventually led to a corner where the crucifixion scene was depicted.

Brought up in a church that viewed religious icons as idolatrous, my mind was conditioned only to think in terms of the correctness of an empty cross, rather than one where the figure of Christ was still on it. Jesus is risen, I was told, and it is true of course. To have a figure of a suffering Christ on the cross was therefore a sign of defeat. So non-Catholic churches inevitably have an empty cross (that looks almost sterile) depicting the fact that Jesus is no longer dead.

However, I have started to look at the cross in a different way to how I was conditioned to look at it. I now see a cross with the figure of Christ still on it not as a symbol of defeat, but as a powerful reminder of his suffering. In the middle of today's feel-good Christianity, it is perhaps all the more important that we meditate on the suffering of Jesus on the cross and what the cross symbolises. We are poorer in our experience and understanding if we rejoice only in the victory his resurrection brings and neglect the cross, a symbol of anguish and suffering. When there had been an opportunity to meditate on the cross – like I did one time in the castle overlooking the Port of Napoli in Italy, in the chamber filled with crosses several centuries old, I would be overwhelmed by a powerful sense of the Lord's presence – this inevitably led to worship. I believe true worship must never be devoid of the message of the cross! We need to be reminded that suffering comes before joy, and crucifixion before resurrection.

In Jordan, I had the opportunity of asking the group gathered what the cross meant to them. One said the cross meant identification – Jesus identifying with us, sinful people. Another said, 'I could have been in his place.' All of us deserved judgment but Jesus took it upon himself. To one brother, the cross meant 'to understand the fellowship of his suffering.' Associating the cross with sacrifice was not lost to the group. The last suggestion was that the cross was counter-culture; that it was foolishness and weakness. Yet God turned it into the greatest symbol in all of history. The meaning of the cross is inexhaustible. It is unique to Christianity. Take that away, and there is nothing left. Christianity is chronically deficient without the cross.

Interestingly, in their account of the crucifixion, the four Gospels are economical in their description of the suffering of the Saviour. We do read some statements spoken by Jesus from the cross expressing his anguish and pain, but not to the extent that we read in Isaiah, particularly in chapters 52 and 53. It is beyond mathematical probability that anyone can predict with some degree of accuracy the near future, but in Isaiah, we get a vivid description of the suffering Saviour foretold several hundred years in advance. Of course, we know now that Isaiah wrote with divine inspiration and revelation.

It is often to these chapters in the book of Isaiah that I go in order to contemplate on the wonder of the suffering Saviour. From its pages, I have a greater appreciation of the full impact of Jesus as fully human (just as he is fully divine). His humiliation in becoming a man and subjecting himself to those limitations is beyond our human finite comprehension. Yet, God in his infinite wisdom carried out his purpose through the incarnation. It is impossible not to be inspired to worship each time. Let me highlight excerpts from Isaiah 42, 49, 52 and 53 that give us an insight into the strength of character and physical description of the Saviour as the Son of Man:

> He will not shout or cry out, or raise his voice in the streets.

A bruised reed he will not break, and a smouldering wick he will not snuff out.

. . . he will not falter or be discouraged

. . . to him who was despised and abhorred by the nation, to the servant of rulers

Just as there were many who were appalled at him – his appearance was so disfigured beyond that of any man and his form marred beyond human likeness –

He grew up before him like a tender shoot, and like a root out of dry ground.

He had no beauty or majesty to attract us to him, nothing in his appearance that we should desire him.

He was despised and rejected by men, a man of sorrows, and familiar with suffering.

Like one from whom men hide their faces he was despised, and we esteemed him not.

Surely he took up our infirmities and carried our sorrows, yet we considered him stricken by God, smitten by him, and afflicted.

But he was pierced for our transgressions, he was crushed for our iniquities; the punishment that brought us peace was upon him, and by his wounds we are healed.

We all, like sheep, have gone astray, each of us has turned to his own way; and the LORD has laid on him the iniquity of us all.

He was oppressed and afflicted, yet he did not open his mouth; he was led like a lamb to the slaughter, and as a sheep before her shearers is silent, so he did not open his mouth.

By oppression and judgment he was taken away. And who can speak of his descendants?

For he was cut off from the land of the living; for the transgression of my people he was stricken.

He was assigned a grave with the wicked, and with the rich in his death, though he had done no violence, nor was any deceit in his mouth.

Yet it was the LORD's will to crush him and cause him to suffer, and though the LORD makes his life a guilt offering, he will see his offspring and prolong his days, and the will of the LORD will prosper in his hand . . . and he will bear their iniquities.

. . . because he poured out his life unto death, and was numbered with the transgressors.

For he bore the sin of many, and made intercession for the transgressors.

(NIV)

Speaking in such detail about someone whom he had never met, the prophet Isaiah must have been baffled. But we have the benefit of history, and therefore the privilege of knowing about what and whom he was speaking. With this knowledge, we are able to cultivate an intimate relationship with the Lord Jesus.

As a Christian, whether old or young, it is important to know what Jesus means to you. Yes, you may know him as God, but have you known him as a Person? Without knowing him personally, Christianity will be an impersonal and detached religion, and your theology, an incomplete one. But when you do know him, you will begin to appreciate a whole new dimension of what a wonderful Saviour he is indeed.

Let me share with you what I know of him as a Person. Much of what I say is not new, but I hope it will get you thinking about what he means to you in personal terms.

## His unwavering courage

I always marvel at the way Jesus handled opposition in the Gospels. He faced opposition head on. He was not intimidated by numbers or by human authority. He did not cringe in fear when threatened by man or nature. He did not mince his words in dealing with opposition (check out Mt. 23 for a full blasting he gave to teachers of the law!). He did not shirk from the threats to his life, from impending death and from eventual execution. If only we had a fraction of this kind of courage! It is foolish and blasphemous of contemporary writers and film directors to depict him as anything less than what he really was. In studying the Scripture, the character of Jesus that emerges is hardly one of weakness. There is nothing but strength in his character.

## His unmatched wisdom

His words are life-giving and life-changing. He does not beat around the bush (when dealing with the woman with a haemorrhage in Mk. 5); he speaks forthrightly with the woman at the well (Jn. 4), and he deals compassionately with the woman caught in adultery who is going to be stoned to death (Jn. 8). The dialogue in each of these incidents is full of wisdom and insight. I never cease to be amazed at Jesus' response to accusations and questions. The wisdom in which his responses are formulated, often in the form of parables, is accurate, relevant, applicable and tight – opponents did not stand a chance even if they dared to challenge him. No man is able to use the words that Jesus used, unless such a person is divinely enabled. What impresses me so much about Jesus is that he used so few words to say so much.

Words were minimal but the impact was great. We are often the opposite – if we are not understood, we talk and talk in the hope of getting ourselves understood. If Jesus was not understood, it was because the disciples or the crowds were too thick in the head to get it.

## His absolute loyalty to followers

Much can be said about the disciples during their three years working and walking with Jesus, and we may be forgiven for thinking in negative terms. When it was time for the crucifixion, they cleanly abandoned their leader. Yet, from a bunch of failures, they became an outstanding group who laid their lives on the line for their Master. Jesus had everything to do with it. He restored all of them and used them powerfully to accomplish his purpose in the church. His loyalty to them was absolute. In his parting words, he told them, 'And surely I am with you always, to the very end of the age.' (Mt. 28:20, NIV) With such a promise and guarantee, small wonder that the first disciples were able to impact their world. And I believe the same assurance is also given to us. We have a living, active and loyal Saviour on our side.

## He is a man of sorrows

Jesus' sorrow is not the brooding kind. It is not like ours. Our sorrow is either self-inflicted, self-centred, or over someone or something close to us. His sense of sorrow is of the deepest kind only he, as God, could bear. Mere human beings would be crushed bearing his load. We need to realise the ugliness of sin and the judgement God the Father will exact on humanity. Jesus took upon himself the judgement of sin for all times and ages, past, present and future. With this immense load, it is not surprising that he was described as 'a man of sorrows, and familiar with suffering' by Isaiah (53:3). His sense of sorrow is because of us and for us. This must be the most comforting characteristic of Jesus. People suffering from pain, sickness, disease, homelessness, statelessness and unfair imprisonment will find in Jesus an ally and a kindred spirit, for he feels sorrow for them. If you are suffering pain so unbearable that you feel no one understands or cares, be assured that there is One who does. Don't forget, he suffered the most excruciating, prolonged form of execution to prove it. He knows, he cares and he bears it with you. There is no pain and no hurt so deep that he cannot understand. Isaiah said, 'by his wounds we are healed.' (53:5).

## His wit and humour

I hope I am not committing sacrilege by suggesting that as a Person, Jesus was witty and had a wholesome sense of humour. I have often wondered why children found it easy snuggling up to him. If Isaiah's description is correct – that physically he was unattractive (see Is. 53:2), then what was it that drew the children to him? If it was not his appearance, then it must be the strength of his personality and character. I believe Jesus was the most winsome Person to all his friends. There are so many accounts in the Gospels that if we were to read them with a candid twist, we will see the humour. Take the incident of turning the water into wine at the wedding in Cana (Jn. 2) – Jesus' timing and gesture was spot on. He added to the hilarity at the wedding. Then imagine the five loaves and two fish the disciples used to feed the five thousand – can you see the expression on the faces of those present staring in amazement, with mouths agape at the 12 basket-loads of leftovers? I can almost see the smiling satisfaction of our Lord as he watched the happy faces of the disciples on seeing yet another miracle. I am amused each time reading the account of the two disciples on the road to Emmaus (Lk. 24) – how the Lord carried the extended conversation with them without disclosing his identity too soon! I simply love the witty side to our Saviour.

## His simplicity in living

I get the impression that materially, the Lord Jesus lived a very carefree existence. His life is uncluttered with things. He could enjoy a fabulous meal at the wedding in Cana – he added value to the merriment with the most outstanding wine (probably the best vintage the world had never known!); or he could go without food for days.

Food to him was secondary, for he once said to his disciples, 'My food . . . is to do the will of him who sent me and to finish his work.' (Jn. 4:34) It sounds as if the Lord was a workaholic – preferring work to food, but in reality, food was a distraction in this incident (ever wondered why in this story – Jesus speaking to the Samaritan woman at the well – it needed 12 men to buy lunch?). He would also dine with those in high society, or with the marginalised, if only to drive home powerful messages of his kingdom. Once he chided Martha for being preoccupied with practical details of house keeping and preparing a meal (see Lk. 10:38-42). He was the guest of honour at her home, but he was not expecting anything special; he was not 'high maintenance'!

He also challenged those who were serious about following him (for there were probably many who were only after him for free meals and free medical treatment!) that 'Foxes have holes and birds of the air have nests, but the Son of Man has nowhere to lay his head.' (Mt. 8:20, NIV) On the one hand, he told serious followers that he would provide no earthly guarantee, and on the other hand, he would promise those who trusted in him that they would lack nothing. His simplicity is a great challenge to my own lifestyle – I want to hold on to material possessions with an open hand instead of a tight grip.

## His selfless life

Readers will notice in the biblical accounts that Jesus never once acted, talked, taught or thought selfishly. His earthly life was always one of giving, serving and putting others before self. Philippians 2:7 says he 'made himself nothing' (NIV), and in another version of the Bible (NASB), it is said he emptied himself. We know as God, his resources are unlimited. But because he was also 100 per cent human, he was subjected to the limitations that press upon a human being. He did experience tiredness, hunger, joy, sadness, and the full range of human emotions. He was intensely tempted but never once succumbed to temptations of the most devilish kind. People took advantage of him, criticised him, sneered, insulted, abused, threatened and laughed at him. He bore it all because of his selfless love for us. Put ourselves next to Jesus, and we are embarrassingly selfish and self-centred. How we need to bless, serve and minister to others like him.

## His obedience as a son

As a son to his earthly parents, the Bible has little to say. But as the Son to his heavenly Father, there is much written – all of which depicts what a perfect Son Jesus was. His obedience was all any father could hope for in a son. To the heavenly Father, his perfect obedience evoked so much pleasure that the heavenly Father could not contain his delight but broke through the heavens to voice his pleasure: 'This is my Son . . . with him I am well pleased.' (Mt. 3:17) The Father did it not once, but twice – once at Jesus' baptism and the second time at the transfiguration, both times before the greatest test took place – that of his obedience unto death by crucifixion. It seemed that the Father had no doubt whatsoever about his Son's absolute obedience when the crunch came. It was enough that he left the magnificence and majesty of heaven to come to grimy and sinful earth. Can we not learn obedience from Jesus? Unfortunately, godly obedience is hard put to the test in an age of rebellion, anti-authority, disobedience and of personal rights and liberties.

## He is a man of his word

Jesus warned his disciples against the hypocrisy of the teachers of the law in Matthew 23:3, 'do everything they tell you. But do not do what they do, for they do not practise what they preach.' Failing to practise what one preaches is hypocrisy. Inconsistency in what we say and what we do borders on hypocrisy. This is a great challenge to all of us. In the earlier days of my being a father, my young children had the natural ability to test and challenge their dad's inconsistency. I confess that many times I caught myself falling short. It was reality therapy for me to wake up to this real challenge of being a man of my word. In Jesus, I find a man true to his word. He did what he said and he lived what he taught. He walked the talk and he talked the walk. Not a single person could fault Jesus for his life and his actions. Consider this – none of those who opposed him dared challenge him even after he had given them a dressing down, for he spoke the truth (opponents would rather resort to the cowardly act of bringing false accusations against Him). Not only was he impossibly wise, he lived an incorruptible life. No man in history had ever lived like Jesus. Just as he did what he said, you can be sure he will do what he has promised. Every single promise he made will come to pass. If you find some promises in the Bible, and for some reason they meet your circumstances and your need in your particular context, you can be sure he will carry it through for you (even if it may not be in your lifetime!).

## He is God

Several years ago, while preparing an Easter message, I was suddenly jolted by the thought that God died on the cross! I was stunned. I never saw it that way before. I had sung hymns about Jesus dying on the cross and I had read books about the cross. I thought I had an idea about the cross, until that moment when it dawned on me that on the cross, God actually died. Just think and ponder for a while this incredible and stunning truth. Jesus. God. Died. Cross. Without true faith in Jesus Christ, it is not surprising that non-believers would find such an act offensive to the point of ludicrous. How can God die? No wonder the Bible says, 'the message of the cross is foolishness to those who are perishing, but to us who are being saved it is the power of God' (1 Cor. 1:18). Non-believers may ask – How can God die for us? It is impossible. But true believers can only exclaim – How can God die for us!!

Do you get it? Have you caught on? The Saviour Jesus, the second Person of the Trinity, God, died on the cross. Christians know he died for us – pray we will never tire of this reminder of our salvation. If per chance you do not know Jesus as Lord and Saviour, now is as good a time as any to acknowledge him by acknowledging your need of him. Turn from your way (for this is what the word 'repent' means) and follow the way of Jesus. Make this commitment to the greatest Man who ever lived; the greatest Man who ever died.

He says to you, 'Come, follow me.' He wants to be your Leader, your Saviour and your Friend.

# Chapter Three

# Starting right

I was converted twice – first to Christ, then to the church!

When I first started off as a Christian, I was unprepared for what lay ahead of me. I thought having believed in Jesus, everything would fall into place. In some ways, some things did fall into place later in life. If life for a young Christian was not perplexing, then it was certainly confusing. I was literally thrown into the deep end of the Christian and church culture.

Some well-meaning Christians will tell you that once you have become a Christian, all your worries and anxieties will disappear. They say the gospel is good news and so it can only mean good. Believe in God and all your troubles will be taken care of. Your problems with alcoholism, addiction to drugs, with gambling, your attraction to pornography, bad and sinful habits will all simply go away, overnight. If only this were true. There are beautiful exceptions of course. The reality is, we still battle with some of these cumbersome sinful habits, simply because we are still sinful human beings. Romans chapter 7 will help you understand the ongoing battle that still takes place in much of life. Thank God that he salvages what seems to be hopeless lives in hopeless situations.

I heard the story of a young man who was sentenced to hang for drug crimes. While on death row, he came to faith in Jesus. But for his crime, he was still hanged. His sin was forgiven and he went to meet his Saviour, but he still had to suffer the consequences of his actions. While it is true that we are made new and whole spiritually, it does not spare us from suffering the consequences of our sins. So be careful when naïve Christians promise you the moon!

Other equally well-meaning Christians will insist that as a Christian, you are not allowed to dance, listen to pop songs (unless it is classical), drink alcohol, smoke, go to the movies (not even when they are squeaky clean), have long hair (except for women), wear jeans, put on make-up, sport metal-studs and so on. Do not laugh; this is still being said! This list of do's and don'ts was either subtly or intentionally handed down from the previous generation, and it is being handed down to the next. We deceive ourselves if we think that in being 'disinfected', we become better Christians. The gospel and the impact of God's grace cut a lot deeper in our life than the externals. If we insist that Christians should be sanitised, rather than sanctified, we only perpetuate a shallow Christianity and a superficial faith bordering hypocrisy. This will only turn others away from the church and from Christ. No wonder people shy away from Christians and the church. Christians can be embarrassingly weird, and when we focus on externals we can be in danger of that. God is more interested in the heart, the inner life, than in external appearance.

Then there are other well-intentioned Christians who will tell you that you must now 'live like a Christian'. This is easier said than done. Ask ten Christians this question – what does it mean to live as a Christian? – and you will probably get ten different answers. How do you 'live like a Christian'? Who sets the standards? Is there one answer for all, or are there 'different strokes for different folks'?

When Christians say this, they are normally implying that you need to live like them, dress like them, look like them and talk like them. You even acquire a whole new vocabulary, new habits, new hobbies and so on. As a matter of fact, you are quite proud of the fact that friends give you a quizzical look when you use impressive old English words like thou, thee, thine, doeth, saith, speaketh, sinneth especially when you pray. Your non-Christian friends and family members are baffled by what is happening to you, while all the time you are quite pleased that God is doing a wonderful work in your life. Without realising it, you become irrelevant, out of place and clueless as far as the real world is concerned. Make sure you are not trapped into taking this route which leads to nowhere in particular.

Then there is the risk that you may end up in an exclusive church. Basically, this spells t-r-o-u-b-l-e. Exclusivism is dangerous. Unfortunately, there are such churches around and they are closer than you think! A church that is exclusive thinks it has a monopoly on the truth. They are proudly convinced, no matter how humble they claim to be, that they are the only ones left in the world who possess the truth, who know right from wrong and who are capable of doing right. It is only to them, or more specifically to the pastor, that God speaks and reveals his truth. They may claim to be like the original New Testament church except that they are more original! Others are considered deviant, off the mark, and to be blunt, hell-bound. Such churches may even be cultic, but they would deny it. Their leaders exert control over members with their rules and personality. They are intolerant towards other churches and Christians. Their members are always suspicious and critical about others. Unfortunately, new and young Christians do end up in such churches. Pray that you will not end up in an exclusive church. If you do, you may want to get out fast!

Take your time in joining a church. Most major denominations are all right. Some independent churches are outstanding. Go along with a Christian friend to find out what their church is like. Ask questions. Don't be intimidated by the church, its structure, its leaders and members. You have the time and the right to decide what you want. Once you are comfortable with a church, make a commitment to attend regularly. Get involved in the church life. Church-shopping is all right in the beginning, but once you have settled for one, do not church-hop. If however there is a need to change church, do so by all means. Christians change churches all the time and for all kinds of reasons. It is better to change church than to drop out of it altogether.

There are other kinds of churches that teach the 'health and wealth' gospel. These churches emphasise that God wants you rich and healthy all the time. The problem with this teaching is that life does not often measure up to it – because sickness, suffering and death take place every day, even to the most sincere and godly Christians. Such teaching, while acceptable in affluent societies, is not much help in poverty stricken countries.

Having had my fair share of exposure to churches of all types and denominations (this term describes a group of churches sharing the same mission, practices and doctrine – of which there are no less than 24,000 around the world!), I would like to share with you some lessons in the hope that your eyes will be wide open when you get involved with a church. Whether you like it or not, the church is a very significant entity God uses. The Bible teaches that the church is the 'bride' of Christ. This implies that he is the Groom. At a wedding, the bride and groom become one. Imagine the importance of that when Christ is the Groom of the church, his bride. Mysterious as it is, the church, in all its imperfections, will last forever.

## The Christian Culture

Understanding the church and the Christian culture is a daunting task. It will take a long time and a lot of reading and exposure in order to begin to understand it. As you start out, you may not think it is an issue. But as you grow and as you get to meet more and more of God's people around the world, you will begin to understand what I mean.

The church of Jesus Christ around the world is so big, varied and diverse. It's impossible to understand fully what God is doing in the worldwide church. So don't even try. Suffice to say that you need to keep your mind and heart open to what God is doing. Be careful when you hear generalisations even from Christian leaders about the condition of the worldwide church, and don't make generalisations yourself. Few are qualified to do so.

I once saw a poster that said – 'The more people I meet, the more I like my dog'. It's cynical to view people this way but there is an element of truth in this statement. I thought that the same could be said about Christians – the more we meet them the more we prefer some less problematic pets! But, this does not give us an excuse not to love and accept people the way Jesus did.

Christians from one denomination may not appreciate or agree with the emphases of another denomination. Many independent (normally smaller, or new) churches split from a denomination or from a mother church for this reason. Often strong personalities are involved. This is quite common and happens in every country. I have learned to survive by appreciating God's people from very different backgrounds and from differing religious emphases. The more secure you are in the faith, the more you read and become informed about the churches and about what God is doing, the less you will feel anxious and threatened. As a matter of fact, you may even find reasons to celebrate the diversity. Get exposed to the diverse church cultures, their worship life, music, verbal jargon and appearance. Respect the way each does their 'thing'. For instance, it is acceptable for men to wear shorts and long socks to an Australian church, but this would be totally out of place and deemed offensive in a high Anglican church or in a formal Korean church.

## Legalism

The second thing I want to share with you is about legalism. Even in the nicest church and among the nicest group of Christians, there is bound to be a sprinkling of legalists. The dictionary says a legalistic person is one who adheres excessively to a law or formula. A legalistic Christian is one who adheres excessively to some law, rule or verses in the Bible. During Jesus' sojourn on earth, he spoke against legalism. Ironically the religious leaders of his time were the worst legalists. Unfortunately, legalism has not died.

Not long ago, I came across a brief column in the Newsweek magazine describing the things banned by the Talebans in Afghanistan. I was struck not so much by the legalism as by the absurdity. Items considered subversive by the Talebans include lipstick, nail polish, chessboards, movies, fireworks, fashion catalogues, cassettes, musical instruments, western clothes, greeting cards with pictures of people, computer disks and the Internet. And yet the same can be said about Christian legalists. Will it come as a shock to you to find that there are churches and Christians that have a ban-list not unlike the above? Watch out for the Christian 'Talebans'!

Legalism over-emphasises forms. It insists that you conform to forms. Legalists control others with rules. Their style is characterised by rigidity, inflexibility and often intolerance. Legalism is a close cousin of inconsistency. It is impossible to do what a legalist says 100 per cent. Jesus called such people hypocrites. Another close cousin of legalism is exclusivism. I have written about that earlier. Watch out for legalism in the church and especially in your own life! When legalism rears its ugly head, it is unpleasant, graceless and causes untold damage to the church and the testimony of Christians. Legalism + inconsistency + exclusivism = a deadly toxicity. Stay away from them.

Here is an illustration of how legalism works in the church. Normally it starts with some strong personalities. Throw in some lopsided teaching from the Bible – this means an imbalanced teaching of one aspect of the Bible at the expense of the whole counsel of God. Strong personalities + excessive emphasis, you get control. Control is enforced with rules. If this is still not enough, which often is the case, these rules quickly become doctrines. No one argues with doctrines. The result is that you have a controlled, stifled, restricted group of

Christians. People are hurt and damaged as a result. But it is still better to be hurt and get out of it than to remain and suffer greater hurt.

The gospel of Jesus Christ is a gospel of grace, of hope, love, forgiveness, and acceptance – these are the complete opposite of legalism. Never exchange this fantastic freedom for anything less.

## Sexual purity

We live in a sex-mad world. Sex is everywhere, even in the most conservative religious nations. As long as you have a TV, or a computer, or a video recording machine, you stand a good chance of easy access. Male and female models in suggestive and provocative poses, in semi or full state of undress, will assault you visually. Sex is depicted and used to sell all sorts of products – from perfume, toiletries, clothes, music, CDs, to cigarettes, swimwear, holiday packages and condominiums. Recently, there were two 'boring' commercials on TV – one used cows and the other, pigs. They were selling milk and pork. They were not as 'attractive' compared to the ads that used skimpily clad models. Sex sells and it sells big time. The sex industry is big business. So sex is a 'given' in most movies, lifestyle magazines, TV programmes, books, Internet, cyberspace, posters and even comic books. Titles of popular magazines disclose just as much. Courses, lessons and glossy literature about improving one's sexual prowess and discovering one's sexuality and identity are easily available. So let's face it, sex is here to stay!

While there have been books written on this subject from a Christian perspective, the church as a whole has been relatively silent in giving biblical teaching. Let's see, when was the last time you heard your pastor or a preacher speak on sex? My guess is that it is rare, and more so in a reserved Asian context where we don't even talk about such things in private, much less in public, and certainly not from the pulpit! If we want to be honest and consistent, then we will have to preach the whole counsel of God, including sex. The Bible contains hundreds of verses on this subject, and many stories of sexual failure and fine examples of sexual purity. I am so grateful that God is not silent on this subject. Why should he be silent when sex is in fact his creation!

While some Christians choose to live in denial on this subject, others over-react. For them, the best way is drastic surgery. If TV is the problem, get rid of it. If the Internet is the problem, disconnect the computer. If we are afraid our children will be exposed to such unhealthy influence, we must shield them. If we are not careful, we end up with draconian measures that eventually backfire.

As Christians, we must learn to be frank, open and yet biblical on this subject. We need to do this in order to pass on the right teaching and values to the next generation. We need to reclaim ground in this area. Otherwise, we will miss out and the devil, our enemy, will continue to spread his lies about something that God created as good.

My son Justin turns fifteen this year. Boys of his age are not as uninformed as we imagine. Some of these kids are street-smart. One day Irene, my wife, suggested that it was time I talked to our son about the 'birds and the bees'.

So I did my fatherly duty. When we had the chance, I took him out to have our 'man to man' talk. We started with a movie and a fabulous meal together. Well into the dinner, I popped the question.

'Son,' I said, 'let's talk about sex.'

'Dad,' he responded, 'what do you want to know?'

He was kidding, of course. I wanted him to understand how he was going to develop as a sexual being. I wanted him to realise that there would be changes in the way he talked, behaved and especially in his mood swing. I wanted him to hear it from his dad and his mum, and not from his school friends! I am not a 'sexpert', but I pride myself in knowing at least a little more than his young peers. True enough, he started relating to me the information that was passed on from his friends. They were simply making fun of sex and the opposite sex! That night, I ignored cultural taboos by talking point blank on this subject. I would rather break some rules and have him learn the correct and biblical truth.

At the end of our conversation, he said, 'Dad, perhaps I don't need to know the details now. Not yet anyway.' That was mature thinking on his part. I didn't press but told him that should he have questions, Dad is always there.

In a nutshell, the Bible teaches that sex is good. God gave it to man and woman when he created them. God intended sex to be enjoyed by his children, but this enjoyment is within a boundary – marriage. Outside of marriage, whether it is pre-marital or extra-marital, sex is wrong and sinful. This truth is often lost in our day and age where immodesty, nudity and under-dressing are considered chic, and adultery, acceptable. At the risk of sounding abnormal, it is important that new and young Christians do not waver from this biblical truth. God has a standard that is often violated by the media and celebrities, whose lifestyle conveys the subtle message that sexual sin is fashionable and acceptable. Alas, young Christian couples fall into the same trap. Do not be deceived, sex outside of marriage is outside of God's will.

If you are guilty of this sin, you need to ask God for forgiveness. The good thing about sin is that because it is sin, it is forgivable. This applies not only to sexual sin. Having repented and received forgiveness, you need to be aware that for most of us who continue to be full-blooded sexual beings, the battle will continue to rage. Some people think that once you are married, sexual temptation will go away as quickly as a sneeze. It may be true for a few, but if we are being honest, we need to admit that it plagues the married and the single, novice Christian or veteran in the faith. There are times even as a happily married man, I find the temptation intense. Thankfully, good habits cultivated through the years – like taking regular exercise and accountability to one or two persons – have provided some safeguard. Be watchful in this area – the enemy is prowling around to devour the vulnerable and susceptible Christian.

This section on sex has taken longer than I have expected. It just goes to show how important an area it is in the Christian battle.

## Unattainable standards

This is an area I struggled with as a new Christian. I struggled because spiritual standards were set so high. The standards set by Christians and the church are so high – they seem to be unattainable even for mature Christians, let alone those new in the faith. Can we achieve perfection? Unlikely. Not on this side of eternity anyway. Then where do we get the idea that we need to be perfect?

Books pertaining to the deeper life have always puzzled me. I don't mean to say my relationship with Jesus is shallow. As I mature in Christ, I can more or less figure out most of what Christian authors write, even when they talk about the deeper life. The problem is, it leaves the young Christian starting out in the Christian life high and dry. When writers write about the deeper life, one gets the impression that they are referring to some white haired old saint dispensing mystical truth. Christian writers feel they must come up with something new and something deep each time a book is written, so it is better if it's about an aspect that no one else has ever thought of or taught before. So you get books about getting deeper into Bible study, going deeper in prayer, in meditation, in solitude, getting deeper and deeper in communion, understanding the deeper ways of God, even deeper than God intended it to be! There are no more simple and easy ways to understand anything! As we read deeper and deeper and our knowledge gets more and more '*cheem*' (a Chinese expression for 'so deep that it is basically incomprehensible'), we find ourselves out of our spiritual depth. Then, so says the preacher and writes the writer, and only then, will we experience what victorious living is all about.

Does it sound complicated? It does to me. Without sounding over-simplistic about the Christian life, I dare suggest that our relationship with the Lord and his Son Jesus, is meant to be simple, uncluttered, undistracting, direct, informal, personal, intimate and straightforward. How complicated can talking with the Lord be? Even the prayer Jesus taught his disciples was just a few sentences. (Mt. 6:9-13) Jesus himself said we should not be long-winded and boring in our conversation with him. (Mt. 6:7) He even used children to demonstrate powerfully what he meant by simple trust and faith (Mk. 10:15). It is only adults like us who tend to complicate matters. One preacher I heard told the audience that in preparing his sermon, he came across 54 different views from Bible commentators over one unfamiliar verse in the Bible! If educated commentators cannot even agree, what chance have we ordinary Christians got? This is not to infer that we should get lazy in reading and meditating on the word of God; I really believe God is easier to know (and live with!) than purported by authors and speakers.

I long to hear preachers preach simply, understandably, practically and candidly about the 'deep things' of God. I find that such sermons have a deeper impact in my life. The truths conveyed are attainable, liveable and do-able, with the help of the Holy Spirit in our life and Jesus dwelling in our hearts.

I also long for leaders, preachers and pastors to be consistent in what they say and what they do. Perhaps one of the bigger stumbling blocks to new Christians is when they do not see the relationship between word and deed in the lives of leaders.

The most effective and powerful testimony is one that is honest, practical and down to earth. Mix such qualities with the fruit of the Spirit and you have someone who is real and human enough for others to want to emulate.

## Inadequate answers

Hard questions don't have soft answers.

Put another way, there are no easy answers to life's problems.

When I first started out as a young Christian, I was fervent in my belief but inexperienced in dealing with hard questions. I remember once trying to witness to a friend, only to have her rebut the little I knew. I felt so discouraged and ashamed that I actually wept that night. In hindsight, I could have saved myself from such needless self-pity. However, that incident gave me the determination to find out answers for myself.

That was more than thirty years ago. If you were to ask me the same questions today, I still may not be able to give you satisfactory answers, but at least I can say I understand the questions! As I look up answers to life's questions, I may understand the answers others have provided, but personally, I still could not come to definite conclusions. Rather than fighting it and tearing my hair (what is left of it) in frustration, I am able to live with ambiguity. I think in life you must develop this ability to accept and live with ambiguity, otherwise you will go crazy. The Bible gives answers but often it does not provide the specifics.

What are some of the hard questions? Try these:

Why is there so much suffering in the world? Why do you say God is a God of love when earthquakes and famines kill the innocent by the thousands? What happens to people who have not heard the gospel? Do they go to hell? Isn't it unfair to destine people to hell when they don't even get a chance to hear, let alone believe? Isn't it unfair that the convicted criminal will go to heaven because he repented at the last minute? What about the person he killed? Why is there hell in the first place, when God is love? It simply doesn't make sense. In case you are tempted to think these questions are rhetorical, they are not. Just as a personal testimony, I have wept for many years wondering what has happened to my mother. She died more than thirty years ago and I would like to think she is in heaven but my sentiments may not be in line with my theology. What do I do?

There are books written giving answers to such tough questions. But let me warn you – you may obtain all the right answers, and you may be satisfied mentally and academically, but you may not be truly and adequately satisfied emotionally. When the issues affect you personally, it is harder to accept emotionally what may be theologically correct. In such a situation, I have learned to leave it to God and trust in his sovereignty, faithfulness, justice and righteousness. He is God and he knows exactly what he is doing even though as finite beings we do not. I will not be swayed in my faith and trust in him just because I am not emotionally pacified.

While having lunch with Patrick Johnstone, the author of the missions handbook *Operation World*, a small group of Christian leaders asked how it was possible to determine if a group of people were genuinely saved or not. His answer was 'only the Lamb of God knows all the names written in the Lamb's book of life.'

I pray too that as you wrestle with some of these issues and questions, you will not give up.

## The strange divide

One practice I have come across among Christians is the practice of separating the spiritual from the material. I don't know where Christians get this idea from. Perhaps as human beings, we tend to revolve around what we can see (material and tangible) and we are uncertain about what we cannot see (the spiritual and intangible).

It could well be that we have simply picked up the worldview that separates the physical from the spiritual. In the New Testament, Christians were grappling with this, except that they called it heresy at that time.

What this separation essentially means is that whereas the spiritual is good, the material is bad. Christians with this kind of thinking will tell you that you must do things that are spiritual – like reading your Bible so that you can feed your soul, pray so that your spiritual life is healthy, use spiritual language, engage in spiritual activities in church, think only spiritual thoughts and so on.

These disciplines are not wrong, but exercising them at the expense of the physical and material is. The danger becomes obvious when we begin to apply it to everything in life. We begin to believe that the spiritual is preferred to the secular (or non-spiritual). Often the demarcation is not as neat and tidy as we think. We come to the conclusion that work for the church is work 'for God' and therefore spiritual, but work outside the church, like what most of us are doing, is work for humanity and therefore unspiritual. Taken further, weekdays are separated from Sunday. Why? Because Sunday is the Lord's day, and therefore spiritual. We can do whatever we like or sin however we like on weekdays because they are not the Lord's (by the way, everyday is the Lord's!). We get schizophrenic without realising it! If we are not careful, we will reject anything and everything that is not spiritual. I know of Christians who, because of this warped thinking choose to only do what they think is spiritual, and neglect their duties as human beings. They forget that while they have the spiritual capacity and the spiritual dimension, they are still 100 per cent human, and as such they have to live with their humanity. Much of life is physical and material. God has made us so, and we must not neglect that. Balance is what is needed.

God created Adam and Eve whole, complete, human beings. He created them in his own image. After he made man and woman, He breathed his spirit into them. Adam and Eve were both physical and spiritual beings. As physical and spiritual beings, humanity is complete. It is wonderful to know that God missed nothing in his creation of humankind. We do well to give attention to nurture, and exercise care over our entire humanness. Every part of us – physical, spiritual, mental, psychological and biological – is important.

## Extra-biblical teaching

This heading is a contradiction. Extra teaching in addition to the Bible is obviously unbiblical. That does not mean these extras do not support or confirm what is already true in the Bible.

There are thousands of Christian books available and a young Christian will find it overwhelming. Don't be surprised if you are bombarded with books on subjects that you didn't even know existed. What should one read? How should one exercise care in what one reads? What are the books that will strengthen faith and which are those that will do damage?

Through the years, I have read so many books and listened to all kinds of preachers. I have friends to thank for recommending good books that have contributed to my growth as a Christian. This has been a safeguard of my time and energy. There are many junk books like there are junk foods. It is wise to know what to read. Generally, well-known and balanced authors are a safe bet. But watch out for nebulous titles on questionable subjects even if they claim to be Christian.

I am part of a Bible study group that has done studies of books, topics and issues, using leader's guides and study aids to help us. Weary of reading what others are saying to us, we decided to read and discuss the Bible all on its own. We wanted to see for ourselves what (new) things God would have us learn. Commentaries are left on the shelf, not because we don't find them helpful (they are when we need to know background and when we come across some knotty verses) but because we would rather let God speak to us without the distraction of study aids. We have all read the Bible and are familiar with it, but it is amazing what we can learn collectively as a group with our accumulated knowledge and experience.

Here's a tip – there are Bibles and there are Bibles! What I mean is that there are Bibles meant for readers of eighteen years and above, and there are Bibles for nine-year-olds. I chanced upon this knowledge when talking to an executive of a Bible-publishing house. True enough, after I had done a simple comparison, I discovered that not all Bibles have the same level of English. My point is, you will grow faster only if you understand what you are reading in the Bible. Upgrade your Bible if the one you are using is too simple, or downgrade (no shame to it) if you find the one you are using is way over your head. I use different Bibles interchangeably in order to get the most out of them.

I come to the end of this chapter. What I have shared I trust has made sense to you as you embark on the Christian life. Starting right is important. It is also not too late to backtrack if you have wandered off at some fork along the way.

# Chapter Four

# Growing up

Some people never grow up.

That's scary. Imagine a fifty-year-old Christian walking around behaving like a little kid. This person would look odd, childish and out of place. The scary thing is that there are such people around. And such a person is in all of us!

I know, because I am like that sometimes. I can put up a mature front before an audience, a congregation, in church and in the office, but I cannot hoodwink my wife whom I live and sleep with every day (except when I am travelling) of our married life. She can tell you about the lapses into immaturity and childish behaviour, but she probably won't. And neither am I proud of the occasions when I didn't show more maturity and Christ-likeness as a husband, father and a Christian leader.

In 'Growing up', I want to share some important principles about maturing as a Christian and as a person. As you read, please do not get the impression that I have arrived and have matured to a point where there is a halo above my head. What I am really trying to convey to you are lessons I am learning as I go along in life.

In the process of learning, we grow to maturity. Maturity does not mean you have finally arrived at sainthood. No matter how mature you think you are, or what people think of you, you will still retain a streak of immaturity. But don't be dismayed. I read a commentary on the book of Jonah by the famous R.T. Kendall, in which he said, 'God can use a crooked stick to draw a straight line'.[1]

I like the truth behind this candid statement. None of us will be 100 per cent straight, but that does not stop God from using us for good.

I became a Christian at the age of seventeen. The first few years of my life were spent in getting adjusted to Christianity, church and Christian friends. At twenty years of age, I got involved in missions. I have never looked back since.

I got married at thirty-one. I met Irene while serving on OM. Some readers commented that I didn't say much about my family in my first book. I had deliberately omitted specific references to them, as I did not want to use them as sermon illustrations. This time round, I have their permission and they get to verify what I have written. Irene is similar to me in many ways – her godliness, generosity, concern for others, moderating skills and personality (I hope I am not conceited to suggest I have the same qualities . . .). Some people say opposites attract. To me, opposites do not attract. Opposites are opposites! Where Irene and I defer are in our idiosyncrasies. Please do not laugh, all of us have them! I will not disclose what our differences are except this – she is a collector and I am a discarder. I leave it to your imagination to figure out what this loaded disclosure means. If you have no idea, ask any married couple!

Our children Justin and Marianne are like us. One looks like mum and the other like dad. The one who

---

[1] R.T. Kendall, *Jonah – An Exposition* (Paternoster Press, 1995), 170

looks like Mum acts like Mum and the one who looks like Dad acts like Dad. The one who looks and acts like Mum is not a girl and the one who looks and acts like Dad is not a boy. If there is one thing that characterises my family, it is humour. There is a generous and spontaneous dose of humour in our household and laughter punctuates much of our family time. Events of the day are recounted with candour. It diffuses tension and has a positive effect on our relationship. We have happy kids as a result.

I cannot say enough about the lessons on maturity I have drawn from my kids and Irene. Fathers learn quickly when they commit silly mistakes, and in that I am a fast learner. I have always appreciated their readiness to forgive and to respect me. My children have shown me in all my 15 years as a father, some real insights into the father-heart of God. The extent fathers will go to meet the requests of their children shows the depth of their love for them, not unlike (though unequal to) the love of our Father in heaven for us, his children. I suppose one has to be a father to understand what I am saying.

Let me get on with the five principles of maturity. As I reflected on these principles, I became aware that these were the same principles I formed in the first five years of my service in missions, from age twenty to twenty-five. When young people tell you about the values they are beginning to form in their lives, do not dismiss them. Biblical values can stand the test of time.

**Principle of Maturity No. 1**
**Learn about Jesus and love him**

As a young Christian I listened to a message by Stephen Olford where he challenged listeners to read the four gospels – Matthew, Mark, Luke and John. He said – if you want to know the Saviour, then read the Gospels. So for the next two years, I read the four gospels, over and over again. Olford was right, my knowledge and relationship with the Saviour grew by leaps and bounds. My love and fondness of the Lord brought me into closer intimacy with him. To this day, I talk to him and interact with him as if he is just standing next to me. I didn't know about the concept of practicing the presence of God but I guess I was doing just that. It is refreshing to know I have been on the right track.

I am still reading the Gospels. The more I read, the more I fall in love with the Saviour. It is not the romantic, fuddy-duddy kind of love. But the kind that leads me to admire, adore and worship. I am not ashamed to say that I love my Master. How it can be possible to live without him, I really don't know!

What happens to people in love? Many years ago I heard Manfred Schaller, a German friend who is the chairman of the board governing the ship MV Doulos, preach on this. He said three things about people who are in love – 1. There is never enough time with the one you love. 2. You are always thinking about this person. 3. You are proud of this person and cannot wait to show off this person to friends. Manfred was drawing an analogy of what happens when we say we love Jesus.

The Bible tells us to imitate Jesus, to fix our eyes on him, the author and finisher of our faith. The Bible also teaches us to be Christlike – in our behaviour, character and in everything that he is. This is the path to maturity. If nothing else, this alone will keep us on the straight and narrow. Let me ask you – have you thought of the Saviour today? Have you thought of him this week? The past month? If you have not then there is something wrong in your relationship with him.

Let me add something here about the Holy Spirit's role in our maturing process.

As a young Christian, I was saddened to see Christians and churches divided over the Holy Spirit who is supposed to unite us. Today, the controversy over the Holy Spirit is still raging on in churches in many countries. It is easy to get cynical about the church. But don't. The Holy Spirit is still working in the midst of human weakness. When the Spirit works, it can get messy. The Spirit does not get messy, but people do. Some pray for revival, but revival can be messy. There are beautiful stories and testimonies, but the mess may come in the next generation, or generations after.

When the Holy Spirit works, it will appear confusing. Onlookers were confused in the second chapter of Acts when the Holy Spirit came upon the disciples. If your friends come to a church and say 'I am confused', tell them not to worry. We like it to be neat and tidy – according to our neat theology/church habits – but the Spirit, when He works, can throw a spanner into our order and neatness. Let me give you an example – God heals, right? Then how come good Christians still get sick and die? There was a popular speaker and writer whom God used to heal many. He died of cancer and a combination of several illnesses. How do you explain that? At the end of the day, we have to admit that we do not know how the Spirit works.

The Holy Spirit is essentially holy. It doesn't take a lot of wisdom to know that holiness is required of us. Are we holy? Do we live in purity? What about our conscience? Is it pure? If my conscience is seared, I know it is the Holy Spirit working in me. I came across a piece of humour concerning conscience, it says – 'conscience is what makes a small boy tell his dad before his sister does.' I trust you are quick to recognise the work of the Spirit in your life, and don't act like the boy!

In the Bible we are taught the Spirit is a deposit, a seal, helper, counsellor, reminder and teacher of truth. The Spirit points us to the Son, and the Son points us to the Father. We have such an incredible resource in the Holy Spirit, and yet many of us live as if the Holy Spirit doesn't exist. A prominent minister startled his denomination when he said: 'If the Holy Spirit were completely withdrawn from the church, the work of the church would go straight on as though nothing had happened!' Pray this will not happen in your church, and that it will not happen in your own life.

Let us keep in step with the Spirit. The Bible says live by the Spirit, and you will not gratify the desires of the sinful nature (Gal. 5:16). The Bible also says to be filled with the Spirit – see Ephesians 5:18. When was the last time you prayed this prayer?

### Principle of Maturity No. 2
### Faithful in the midst of failure

Responsibility comes only when we have proven our faithfulness. Greater responsibility comes when we have been faithful in small responsibilities.

A vicar of an Anglican church, serving on the MV Doulos was for some unknown reason assigned to the duty of a receptionist. In addition, he was given the job as the ship's travel agent responsible for booking air tickets for members and visitors – all mundane work. For any clergy to be assigned to such duties would border on insult. The first months were obviously difficult ones. God taught him a lesson about humility. Then he left the ship to return home to settle some family matters. When the time came for him to return to the ship, he resisted and fought against it. Everything about the ship was bad and he refused to go back to the same. But God wanted him back. Eventually, he experienced a change of heart. God broke through to him. When he got back to the ship, there was a complete about-turn in everything. This time round, everything looked so good. What made the difference? There was a change of attitude. God was more concerned about the heart.

How faithful are you? Or, how loyal are you? Faithfulness and loyalty are related words. Many issues in life hang on your faithfulness and loyalty. If you are faithful to the Lord, it overflows into other areas of your life. If you fail in your faithfulness, they are affected as well. How faithful are you in discharging your church responsibility? How faithful are you in your marriage? Marriage lately has taken a battering. Many Christian marriages are wrecked because one spouse is unfaithful. What about faithfulness in your work? Are you known for your diligence and loyalty, in your company? Job-hopping has become the norm, but it has its consequences. Are you able to stay faithful to the Lord if you are discouraged and criticised? If you are going to live on planet earth, you better get used to discouragement and criticism. Often, criticism is more perceived than real. Our imagination regarding what others say or don't say about us spins out of control. I like this insightful observation *'Don't worry about what people think of you, they seldom do!'* Here's another one – *'What you hear never seems as exciting/depressing as what you overhear.'*

If you have never had criticisms levelled at you – try preaching! I guarantee that you will get some in no time. Well-meaning criticism is reality therapy!

Don't be afraid to fail either. In Germany not long ago, some young people committed suicide because they failed in their exams. We hear of such stories also in Hong Kong and Japan. Singapore, where I live, is not spared. One of the most heartbreaking stories is about a twelve-year old girl who jumped from a high-rise public housing block, not because she failed, but because she was afraid her parents would be angry with her for not doing well enough! My heart ached as I listened to her father on TV – he was in the depths of anguish. Although my children did quite well that same year, I assured them that as long as they had given it their best shot, it didn't matter to me if they failed. I wanted them to know that failing an exam was not worth dying for! Several times since, one of them has failed in some subjects. As a parent, I was honestly pleased that he had the opportunity to learn from failure. We had already noticed those who did well were getting snobbish. And there's nothing like failure to learn some humility and empathy towards others who fair worse.

I like the common experience we all share *'If at first you don't succeed, you are about the same like everyone else.'* Failure is normal. It is nothing new. *'But,'* continues this humorous statement, *'don't try to parachute.'*

Unfortunately, some societies are intolerant with those who fail. Our society is fascinated with success. You see it in almost all the media, in the system of education, in countless books on all kinds of subjects on how to succeed, in magazine features, and in the way society rewards the successful.

How does an average society measure success? Beauty is one way. If you are not convinced, just check out popular fashion and magazines. In their natural appearance the front cover personality or celebrity is beautiful enough. With computer touch-ups, teeth sparkle, blemished skin turns silky and thinning hair can look full and coiffed. The final printout looks more perfect than the person really is. It is illusionary but buyers don't usually give a second thought. Skinny bodies are another measure of success. Models, with bodies that look anorexic, give the impression that they have an eating disorder but people may think they are perfect. Male models – usually fit and muscular hunks communicate the same message. Another measure is numbers: the bigger the number, the more successful a person or a programme is. Transfer this value to the church, what do you get? Christians from big churches usually talk with a sense of pride concerning the size of their churches and the size of the churches' budget. Status is yet another measure. Where your house is located, the make of your car, the friends you meet, club membership and your position in the corporate world are all symbols of success. I am not saying all these are wrong (some of my friends have all of these) but do not mistake them for success. Some people may be successful as far as status is concerned, but they may be utter failures in family and private life. You read it every day in gossip columns!

Is God impressed with our success? The answer is obvious. I am always impressed by the example of Jesus. He would not qualify to grace the covers of male magazines. If you measure Jesus by the way we measure success, then he was a failure. Why? His close companions left him, He apparently lost his cause, he was ridiculed, mocked, spat at, and was finally executed like a common criminal. What a way to die!

If looks and achievements do not impress God, then what will? What then is true success? True success comes with humility, and obedience to Jesus Christ. Jesus possessed these same qualities.

It doesn't matter if you fail, as long as you are obedient and humble. It is all right to fail! Allow room for failure. We are sinners – as such, we shall sin and fail every day. We need to confess and repent every day. Most of us don't set out to fail. But if we do, trust the Lord to salvage our failures, even if it is due to our stupidity! His grace makes the difference.

It is funny to say this – don't be boastful about failure. It is a weird sense of pride that is proud of our failure, yet some people feel this way. It is like saying you are quite proud of your humility! Either way, when we think and act this way, we stand in danger of becoming judgmental and jealous towards those who are successful. This is something we need to guard against.

## Principle of Maturity No. 3
## Esteeming and forgiving others

Philippians 2:3: '. . . Let each esteem other better than themselves' (KJV) is one of the trademark verses that is easy to understand and hard to do. Pride often stands in the way of esteeming others.

To esteem others means you regard, favour, and prefer others more highly than yourself.

In practical terms, it may mean recognising that other people's ideas are far better than our own. It may infer the ease we have in accepting better ideas. Even with lousy ideas, if the attitude is to esteem, we must be accepting, and pray and hope for the best.

In serving the Lord and in my travels, I have come to realise that my culture is not always the best! Of course there are good points, but there are bad ones too. Others can tell the level of our maturity by the way we handle criticisms levelled at our country, people and culture. We must be slow in criticising other countries if we do not like our own criticized, and learn to esteem other cultures better than our own. If we are guests in another country, it is impolite to badmouth the host country, yet I often see missionaries making this mistake. We do not like that if visitors say the same of us, so it augurs well to zip up our lips if we are tempted to talk badly about them.

It is a biblical injunction to respect and be courteous towards others. For this reason, we must make every effort to disregard racial prejudice. Prejudice is ugly, and racial prejudice tops the list. Carried to an extreme you get race supremacists. As Christians, there should not be cultural, racial and religious pride and prejudice. We will be naïve to think that this does not happen in the church of Jesus Christ.

When we think about esteeming others, we think naturally of those worthy of our esteem, or those who are older. We need to learn to esteem people regardless of their age. Do you find it easy to esteem children? Jesus did. Paul said that we as fathers should not exasperate them. (See Eph. 6:4, NIV) What about esteeming others whom we do not agree with? What do Christians do when they disagree? Leave the church – or worst, split the church! Someone candidly said, 'When two Christians gather together, there is a church; when three gather together, there are two churches!'

Esteeming others is a proactive way of staying humble.

Do you find it easy to forgive those who have offended you? It is easy to give a quick yes as an answer to this question. But think for a minute. Most of us wrestle with some form of unforgiveness in our life. I include myself. It takes the will to say you want to forgive when unforgiveness creeps into your heart. Some people seem to have final victory over this issue. But if my guess is correct, unforgiveness makes a comeback every now and then, perhaps triggered by some memory or incident. At such times, we need to exercise the will to forgive. The Bible does indicate that forgiving someone can be a repetitive exercise. (See Mt. 18:21,22) Then there are those whom you have offended. The right thing to do is to ask for forgiveness when the first opportunity arises. Restoration and reconciliation of relationships is a powerful and positive experience and testimony.

What happens when you choose not to forgive? An unforgiving spirit will only gnaw at you. If not dealt with, you will be consumed. It is like a disease. Left untreated, it spreads. It affects your prayer life and it causes you to be spiritually deaf to God and to others. Not only are you setting yourself up for more difficult time ahead, your family suffers silently the resentment and bitterness that stem from your unforgiving spirit. As a result, you grieve the Holy Spirit, whose influence on you will only decrease.

## Principle of Maturity No. 4
## Always give thanks and pray

Philippians 4:6 says 'Do not be anxious about anything, but in everything, by prayer and petition, with thanksgiving, present your requests to God. And the peace of God, which transcends all understanding, will guard your hearts and your minds in Christ Jesus.' (NIV)

I didn't know what a worrier I was until I was in the hot seat of leadership. With leadership comes responsibility. When you *are* responsible and you *feel* responsible for people and situations, it can be a real worry. Jesus' instruction to his disciples in Matthew 6:25-34 concerning the futility and silliness of worry is a must-read. You will benefit from the full importance of what he is saying. I have come across all sorts of seminars offering answers and solutions to combat anxiety, worry and stress, but I have yet to come across a more succinct, logical and practical solution to worry than what Jesus prescribes in this passage.

Are you anxious? Are you a worrier? In the Matthew passage, Jesus said, 'do not worry' – three times. If Jesus deemed it necessary to repeat it twice, then I want to do exactly as he said. Yet, as human beings, we prefer to worry. It is easier to worry. We think by worrying we have a better feel and control of the problem. How stupid can we get. Between worrying and not, most people will choose the former!

Jesus said not to worry – a passive instruction, and added an active phrase 'seek first his kingdom' (verse 33). I remember reading this passage when I was seeking the Lord at the age of nineteen as to what I should do with my life. It was staring at me for several weeks when I finally got it. With that confidence, I committed my future to him. Not quite sure what his kingdom was I thought I would seek him first anyway. After all, he is the King in his kingdom. That was thirty years ago. I want to testify that Jesus has kept his promise to me. He is still providing for my family and for me. It has also taken me years to learn not to worry, and it does not come easily.

Two effective ways to deal with worry and anxiety are praying and thanksgiving. In praying, we are acknowledging our dependence on God; in thanking, we acknowledge in faith his provision and his answers to all our needs. These two disciplines (it does take discipline) are key to experiencing the peace of God in the midst of uncertainties. And I propose that the reason many of us do not have peace is that we don't pray enough and thank God enough.

Praying and thanking God are acts of faith. They pave the way to contentment – and the Bible says 'godliness with contentment is great gain' (1 Tim. 6:6, NIV). In all the years of service, I have found God to be absolutely faithful. It does not mean that all my prayers are answered, but it does mean I know he hears me.

I was stark broke after the first ten years serving on OM. In OM, like in many organisations, members are to trust the Lord to provide for all their personal and ministry needs. Few complained as we saw in this lifestyle our desire to honour him in our dependence. I remember living from hand to mouth for a period of my life, in Bangladesh, then in India and in several other places. Even when I was leading the work in Singapore, I avoided over-indulgence and so limited myself to a frugal budget of S$1.50 per meal. Plus travel and some essentials, my budget was S$150 per month. There was nothing left to save for a rainy day. When it came time for me to propose to Irene, I knew for sure she was not going to marry me for my money! As a matter of fact, I was quite apprehensive about Irene's father's response when I asked him for the hand of his daughter – would he consent to the marriage or would he reject me? At that point, I had neither the wealth nor the assurance of financial security. To my utter surprise, Irene's father never grilled me with questions about money. He simply said yes after being assured that his daughter would have a roof over her head. It is understandable for a father to be protective of his daughter, and what a risk he took in allowing his highly educated daughter to marry a poor missionary. I will always remember fondly my father-in-law who had since been promoted to glory, and my mother-in-law, for their graciousness. In his faithfulness, God provided every single cent for our wedding and enough for an initial deposit on a public housing block flat that is now our home.

Gratitude has a flip side, and it is generosity. God is a giving God. I know this is stating the obvious and this cliché stands in danger of being trite from overuse. God is perfectly generous. If you think God is a miserly God who delights in withholding his goodness and blessings from us, then you are probably mistaking him for someone stingy!

God's generosity is beautifully depicted in the act of giving his Son. No one in all history has been able to adequately fathom what this act of generosity means. What is more, instead of judgment, we who are believers are going to share as heirs in his kingdom.

I learnt a simple lesson from my daughter on my last birthday. Marianne asked me for S$10. When I asked her what it was for, she replied, 'I want to put it in an *ang-pow* to give it to you for your birthday.' *Ang-pows* are red envelopes containing cash the Chinese give to one another on auspicious occasions. She asked me for money in order to give it to me as a gift! Smart girl. Without sounding sacrilegious, Marianne did to me what God normally does to us. He gives us so that we can give to him. Conversely, he asks from us but invariably returns to us, perhaps not in kind but in every spiritual blessing.

It does not make sense when Christians are stingy, possessive and over-calculative. Sure, they can disguise such traits with acceptable words like 'thrift', 'good stewardship', 'frugality', but these hardly convince anyone. Such Christians often forget what God has done for them. The Bible talks about hilarious giving – 'God loves a cheerful giver' (2 Cor. 9:7, NIV). When we realise how much God has given to us, we will want to give.

Let me encourage you in one of the most encouraging ministries you can ever get involved in – it is the ministry of giving. You will experience the joy and the delight in seeing what it does to those who receive. I have seen it in their eyes – they normally well up in tears and gratitude. That is why I love giving. I don't have much, but it does not matter. Don't be intimidated because you can only give a little. God can use any amount and multiply it for His glory.

One word of caution though. It would be a mistake to think that because we give to people and to God's work, everything will be fine with us. If we think this way, we are in for a surprise. Being generous in our giving does not guarantee anything. We do it in obedience. When God blesses in return, it is because of his mercy. Having bad things happen to us does not mean God loves us less. On the contrary, God disciplines us because he loves us and ultimately it is for our good. Stuart Briscoe said this in a meeting at a Keswick Convention in Singapore in the seventies (wow, that far back), *'Judgement is getting what we deserve. Mercy is not getting what we deserve. Grace is getting what we do not deserve.'* Ultimately it comes down to God's providence – the basis of why good and bad things happen to the best Christians.

One last thing I would like to tag on to this principle – learn to laugh. I believe laughter is a gift from God. I have seen how laughter diffuses the tension between friends, and certainly between married couples. I have used humour in much of my preaching and relationships. My family is a good example of a laughing family.

## Principle of Maturity No. 5
## Missions in the face of hardship

To the young, timid and budding church leader Timothy, Paul the veteran had this advice in 2 Timothy 2:3 –

'Endure hardship like a good soldier of Christ Jesus.'
(NIV)

Serving God is like soldiering. Having served as a soldier, I can understand Paul's instructions. Soldiering involves the acquisition and development of multiple skills. There is training in discipline, in individual proficiency, in teamwork, in handling of weapons and in a host of physical and mental development. Modern warfare and ancient warfare differ. I suppose ancient warfare was more primitive, crude and slower. Modern warfare can be swift and devastating.

Paul's instruction to Timothy is to endure hardship like a good soldier serving his King. Good soldiers endure hardship, implying that bad soldiers don't. There are soldiers who are lazy and ill disciplined, who contravene orders and commit insubordination. They are no good at enduring hardship like good soldiers. The analogy is that good Christians must endure hardship. How? Like good soldiers. Good soldiers accept what is handed down to them. Good soldiers are always alert. They can do without the luxury of comfort and slumber. They get tired but they endure. When there is a shortage of food, they do not complain. Their interest is to serve their country and their king; to provide safety, protection from the enemy and maintaining the sovereignty of the king. They are willing to endure all these for the sake of the king they serve. For the sake of Jesus their King, Christians must exercise endurance. The King endured the cross, the ultimate hardship, so must his soldiers.

As long as you are on planet earth, you may as well accept that hardship is going to be part of life. Expect it and endure it. We must learn to understand the theology of suffering and pain. There is no education like adversity. And in adversity, we must show courage. A year ago, I hosted Gladys Staines and her daughter

Esther. I got to know Gladys when she was on OM. She met and married Graham and continued their service in the leprosy mission in Orissa, India. Graham and their two young sons were cruelly attacked and burnt alive by religious militants. This horrendous incident was known throughout India and the world. I had followed the news and had kept in touch with Gladys. It was such a joy to have her and Esther visit us. On the Sunday, Gladys consented to speak at my home church. Before she did, I took the opportunity to conduct an interview with her. I had asked her earlier about it and she did not mind as she had already processed much of what took place. The depth of her suffering and pain was surpassed only by the grace and the love of God. As she and Esther shared, their courage in the face of adversity shone through to the congregation. Out of a horrific situation, they were able to forgive. I found out that this same response was televised and broadcast nationwide in India and that had led many to desire the same love and faith that Gladys possesses. As I stood next to them, I felt so small. It was such a powerful testimony and such a moving moment that caused not a few tears. It was indeed a great privilege to hear of such grace in enduring pain and suffering. It made the problems we face look so small and trivia.

Daniel 3:16–18 is one of my favourite passages in the Bible. It's about faith under fire similar to that of Gladys'. 'Shadrach, Meshach and Abednego replied to the king, "O Nebuchadnezzar, we do not need to defend ourselves before you in this matter. If we are thrown into the blazing furnace, the God we serve is able to save us from it, and he will rescue us from your hand, O king. But even if he does not, we want you to know, O king, that we will not serve your gods or worship the image of gold you have set up."' True faith never wavers under pressure. 'Even if [God] does not [save], we will not serve your gods' is a powerful declaration of loyalty. The crunch came for the three friends, and they passed the test. When the crunch comes, I wonder how we will fair. Will we buckle under the pressure or will we stand with solid faith like these great examples?

Let me close with a quote from Peter Kuzmic, when he spoke at my home church. He said this: '*Charisma without character is a catastrophe.*' In the maturing process, what matters most is our character development. Our character is the end result of the maturing process. And maturity comes as we daily put into practice biblical principles like those I have just shared. They have worked for me. I encourage you to develop your own.

If you don't get your act together in life, if you don't begin to work on your character, and if you don't begin to grow up in maturity, chances are you will never grow at all. You stand in danger of becoming yet another church casualty. We are all potential backsliders! It does not take much to backslide – just a little fester, a little unhappiness, a broken relationship, a little resentment, a little anger to start with, a subtle form of pride...

And before we know it, we are a statistic.

# Chapter Five

# Me, a leader?

Yes. You can be a leader.

There are all sorts of leaders. Leaders with dynamic personalities, leaders who lead by example, leaders who serve, leaders who are visionary, leaders who are gifted in administration, leaders who are geniuses and leaders who are movers and shakers. If this is the picture of a leader you conjure up in your mind, then your reluctance to the challenge of leadership is understandable. Few people would measure up to that anyway.

Leadership comes at all levels. As long as you are holding some responsibility, you are exercising some leadership role. As soon as you are a parent, a father or a mother, you become the natural leader of the family, whether you like it or not – and this job is long-term! Young or old, masculine or feminine, God can make a leader out of you.

While some people aspire to be leaders, most don't. Are leaders born or bred? Gurus on this subject tell us leaders are bred, although some leaders may be born with this ability. The upbringing, the conditioning, exposure, culture, parents, teachers and so on, all contribute to the making of a leader. Some leaders simply blossom into leadership while others take a longer time to learn – like most biblical characters. We read about Abraham, Moses, Joshua, David and a collection of them in the book of Judges – all were so different and yet each was greatly used by God. A careful study of each of them will challenge our favourite theories about good leadership. Growing in leadership is a process and it takes time and experience. There is no one set way to lead and many leaders learn leadership the hard way. While we are thankful for the models/formulas of leadership western writers write about, they can either be inappropriate or fall short in a cross-cultural setting. The study of leadership has evolved and comes in a cycle. You may even have some ideas of your own about leadership.

Had someone told me I would be in leadership twenty-eight years ago, I would not have believed that person. When I first set out in life and in missions, leadership hardly entered my mind. The leaders I worked under were simply too intimidating. Most people can be forgiven for feeling this way. When a person badly wants to be a leader, watch out! In the context of biblical leadership, humility is *the* prerequisite! Unless such a person is properly coached, prepared and mentored in godly and biblical leadership, they are heading for disaster, and so are their followers. This does happen. There are enough examples, including recent ones, of leaders who wrecked their lives and the lives of others.

There is no shortage of 'How to' books on leading, on becoming a leader and on leadership, including outstanding ones written by Christians. I am writing here more as a follower than an accomplished leader. I have benefited much from good models of leadership. It has been my privilege to work with a whole range of dynamic, godly, passionate, loving, gracious, wise and ordinary leaders. I pray that whatever nuggets you can glean from this chapter will be helpful in your quest to be a good leader.

Leadership came at a young age for me. I didn't have the benefit of leadership training or orientation. It was a straightforward matter of being thrown into the deep end – and very deep it was too! Of late, I have been providing leadership to the work of OM in East Asia Pacific. We have offices and teams working in 14 countries, all led by nationals. There are as many as 600 from this part of the world serving around the OM world, plus one hundred and forty or so children. Working with me is a team of eight men living in six countries across the region. We are connected electronically but we have never met as a complete team. This is my virtual team. In this day and age, we are leading by telephone and email! There are positives with this kind of leading, but also negatives, especially when we do not see each other face to face.

The great learning curve for me takes place while sharing the leadership with all the national boards, whose members are all leaders in their own right. An average year for me includes a good dose of board meetings that last from several hours to several days. I meet up with the boards of Papua New Guinea, Australia, Japan, Malaysia, The Philippines, Indonesia, Hong Kong, Singapore, New Zealand and South Korea on a regular basis. Embedded in these boards are cultures as different as kimchi is from cheese, and sushi from sweet potato. The leadership culture is also vastly different, from very hierarchical to relational and from democratic to 'buddy' system. Can you figure out what style suits which country? I have developed good relationships with all the chairpersons and most of the board members. This has taken much time and effort. You get an idea of the uniqueness of my job. But don't cry for me, I enjoy my leadership role across cultures.

Many leaders are good followers. Biblical leadership has one very significant and important dimension that worldly (as in non-biblical) leadership does not have. Biblical leadership operates also in the spiritual realm. The Bible has much to say about the influence and the aid of the Holy Spirit in the affairs of the church and of the world. A leader seeking to lead in a biblical way has the Holy Spirit to empower and enable. God, through the Holy Spirit, provides for the shortfall in gifting and ability. Grace comes with the office and responsibility. No leader, if they are speaking biblically, can boast of self-adequacy – this will immediately disqualify one from biblical leadership. Only when we admit our inadequacy will we find in him the all-sufficiency.

Leadership has its upside. God's wisdom is accessible and available – of course this is true for everyone, not just leaders. But I believe God gives wisdom peculiar to leaders in exercising leadership. As with God's wisdom, God's richest resources are also at their disposal. Leaders also have the unusual privilege of influencing and speaking into the lives of others, through their preaching, teaching, writing, or action. Another upside is the privilege of making significant decisions concerning life and ministry. The higher you go in leadership, the greater will be your positional authority. It is an authority vested by God through others – fellow leaders or peers. Needless to say, responsibility comes with the upside.

Leadership also has its downside. Pressure is the first one that comes to mind. This is a given. Get ready for pressure in your personal and family life. Pressure of seeing to the need of personnel and finance – typically the two areas that give the most problems in any work of God – will press on you day and night. The higher up you are in leadership, the hotter the seat! Another downside is that leadership involves a lot of hard work. Peter Maiden, OM's International Director, once said that people are reluctant to become leaders because of laziness. If you are not ready for hard work, then do not be a leader. You will have sleepless nights worrying over problems. You will lose sleep just when you need it most. You will discover pretty quickly that people with problems are not good at organising them to suit your convenience! Conflicts amongst God's people are complicated and complex, damaging and hurtful, but regrettably they happen all the time. Fasten your seat belt and get ready to enter the fray in conflict resolution. If you do not know what I am talking about, you will soon find out!

Why, then, do people want to lead at all? I don't have the full answer. Perhaps we are all wired differently – some aspire to be leaders more than others. Perhaps in God's sovereignty, some are destined to lead – like most leaders in the Bible. Judging by the reluctance of many biblical and life examples, this appears to be the case. Perhaps some enjoy the challenge of leading – or to be truthful, they are not very good at following. Perhaps there are some who delight in the position and authority, the recognition and the privilege. While such 'perks' come with leadership, I would be worried if they were the only motivation. I suppose as human beings, we can never be completely rid of this tendency, even amongst the noblest and humblest of Christian leaders.

Leadership is here to stay. We will always have to live under one leader or another. You can't live without them. This is the way the church of Jesus Christ is organised and governed. If it says so in the word of God, then it is something we have to accept.

Here are some thoughts on leadership.

## Handling criticism

*Newsweek* is one of the popular magazines I subscribe to. I never miss reading the 'Letters' page, featuring brief letters from readers responding to articles in the previous issues. The editor is always objective enough to feature the brickbats as well as the accolades from readers. For every decent article, there is bound to be agreement and objection. Sometimes, the objections can be nasty and intolerant. What amazes me is that regular writers continue to write for the magazine, despite the cutting criticisms. These people must have developed skin as thick as a rhinoceros. They have to in order to survive in the real world of journalism. They deal with criticism like water off a duck's back. And in Christian leadership, one needs to deal with criticism in more or less the same way. It does not take a whole lot of wisdom to know that it is easier to criticise than to be criticised. Everyone has an opinion, and if you were to heed them all, you would go bonkers.

I have often seen leaders mishandling criticism. The criticism may be fair and valid, but they fail to see it that way and take it personally. In response, they become defensive, or worse, angry. The Bible says 'Faithful are the wounds of a friend; but the kisses of an enemy are deceitful.' (Prov. 27:6, KJV) But as human beings, in our desire for affirmation and clamour for recognition, we enjoy the kisses of the enemy more, and become spiteful towards friends with their constructive (albeit, wounding) criticism. Granted, constructive criticism is still criticism, but when it is given in love by an ally, it is positive. Without criticism, we will never learn to improve in our skills and efforts in leading. Pride hinders us from accepting criticism. As leaders, we need to cultivate maturity in handling criticism.

Speaking as an Asian, I observe that we are not very good at accepting criticism and using it to our advantage. Usually, we feel offended when criticised. And when done publicly, it can be humiliating and even the best of allies can become vengeful. This is restricted not only to the political arena; it filters into the church as well. Asians credit themselves for being relational, but the flipside of this is that we are not very good at distinguishing the principle from the person. When an issue or decision is over a principle, the individual feels personal offence. We can learn much from our western counterparts, who are better at distinguishing people from principles. It does not mean that they do not feel offence when criticised – they are just as human, but they do not get offended to the degree like Asians do.

I heard the story of the Kenyan long distance runner who was to face the disciplinary committee at a world athletic meet in Switzerland. This Kenyan was leading in a race, followed closely by his friend and fellow countryman when he slowed down to let his friend pass just metres before the finishing tape. The disciplinary committee smelt conspiracy, but the Kenyan's explanation was something like: 'Well, I won the last race and got the prize. This time it is his turn.' That's how friends treat each other. But sometimes a matter of principle can cut through relationships. Which is right?

## A leader's disciplines

We are all creatures of habit; we are comfortable with familiarity. Every Christian leader I know is a creature of habit. I am referring to godly, spiritual habit. In other words, they are people of discipline. A disorganised, ill-disciplined, disorderly leader is a misnomer.

Though the priority and emphasis may differ, Christian leaders have some given (not optional) disciplines of the physical, emotional and spiritual nature. These disciplines invariably include spending time in personal and corporate/group prayer; the discipline of fasting – this is increasingly neglected in an age of feasting – and the study and reflection on the word of God. In doing these things, we are following none other than the example of the Lord Jesus himself. Most Christian leaders I know have also cultivated a habit of reading. This increases knowledge and information and opens up all kinds of possibilities in the way the work of God is carried out. I would also consider the discipline of learning new things, being open to new ideas, being willing to consider innovation as an important one in this age of technology. If leaders do not adapt and adopt, we will get out of sync and become irrelevant in this modern world.

Another important discipline is the discipline of accountability. As leaders, we cannot afford to operate like a free agent or someone marooned on an island. Without accountability, danger of excess and abuse is doubled or tripled.

Lastly, I would add the discipline of exercise. Leaders needlessly fall victim to sicknesses, strokes and become overweight – things that are often caused by unhealthy eating habits or the lack of discipline in eating. As a result, their leadership lifespan is sadly cut short, to the loss of God's overall work. I believe if leaders were to exercise regularly, they would be physically fitter in the service of God. This point is said tongue-in-cheek, as I am nowhere near old enough to prove this theory though conventional medical wisdom tells us so. The bottom line is a healthy lifestyle.

If leaders fail to exercise basic discipline in some of these areas, they disqualify themselves.

## Leading is serving

Biblical leadership is essentially servanthood. Leaders
worth their salt know this like they know the back of
their hands. Yet, serving in practice is really hard. It goes
against the grain. Non-biblical leaders are served; they
don't serve. They are respected, esteemed and hon-
oured. Asians are especially good at revering leaders,
especially when they are successful and have the personality and the position to go along with it.

Jesus' model of leadership is servanthood. He said
that we should be different from leaders of the world
who lord it over the people they rule; we should serve.
(See Mt. 20:25-28) And of course he led by example – he
wrapped a towel around his waist and started washing
the disciples' feet. (See Jn. 13:2-17) The Master of the
Universe, the King of kings, chose to wash the dirty feet
of sinful men. That's a graphic lesson for leaders who
have allowed the pedestal of leadership to overshadow
the fundamental need to serve. It's not just this incident
– the whole of his life is spent in serving, giving, blessing and sacrificing for others. This is biblical leadership.
If you have to miss anything at all, don't miss this lesson.

## Making hard decisions

A leader exercises authority by virtue of the office or
position. The higher the position held, the higher the
authority. This is positional authority. When a leader
no longer holds the office or the position, they may still
be respected and their views sought, but there is no
longer the authority that the office or position gives,
except perhaps the spiritual authority that the person

may still retain vested from God (but this is true of all believers).

In positional leadership, there are times when you have to make hard decisions. This is particularly so in conflict resolution. One of the most common problems in leadership is resolving conflicts between colleagues and between leaders, the responsibility of which no sane person would desire! But someone has to do it and it becomes the bounden duty of the leader with the position and office. It is always awkward, and seldom will it result in a win-win situation. Church and ministry splits are never pleasant; neither is the breakdown in relationship. Forget the wisecrack about resolving conflicts – that you have to listen to both sides of the story, and the third side, which is the truth. The wise guy who came up with this simplistic view had never been in cross-cultural situations, or in a Christian situation where everyone would tell their version of the truth! And even if you think you understood and have a solution, it still does not resolve the conflict. People are hurt and relationships are broken. This happens all the time. Very often healing does not take place, but when it does, it is still wise to keep people apart. I am sure when we get to heaven, this will all be sorted out, but until then, let's do all that we can as leaders in making hard (and by God's grace, wise) decisions, but be ready to lose some friends.

## Watch out for the danger

Leadership has its danger. The fact that countless Christian leaders have fallen is a warning to all of us. No Christian leader is foolproof. As a matter of fact, just when you think you are doing all right, beware! The enemy is always on the lookout for leaders who drop their guard.

Fame, success, sexual lust and pride are curses in disguise lurking round the corner waiting to pounce on you. They are subtle, attractive and enticing. Any one of these will puff you up to a point where you feel comfortably proud with yourself. In your puffed-up state, you begin to think that there really isn't anything you can't do, and you can certainly manage without God's help. One thing leads to another. Leadership, or its abuse, opens the doors to wealth, to indulgence and often to sexual immorality. It is worrying when news breaks of one more famous Christian leader falling into immorality. When this happens, the testimony of Jesus Christ and Christians receives a severe lashing. Lest we become self-righteous and think that it will never happen to us, take heed. The scariest part is that it can happen anytime! Before you know it, you are caught with your pants down (forgive the pun). The bubble has burst. Often it is the Lord who bursts it. It is because of his mercy that he does it to you. When a leader falls, it is a hard fall. Still, it is never too late to repent and humble yourself before God . . . but if you refuse, the outcome will be tragic. Godly humility and frequent reminders of our limitations is a great antidote against pride and all its close cousins.

Don't say it will never happen to you. After all, you say, I am not a leader. The devil does not care if you are a leader or not. All he cares about is to destroy everything that you have got. Many who boasted are no longer in the ministry; some have faded into oblivion, never to be heard of again.

## Team leadership

Earlier books on leadership portrayed leading as a lonely vocation, and the leader as someone struggling

with loneliness. The loneliness that the lone leader suffered, suggested the writers, stemmed from doing a job
that was misunderstood by others and the pressure that
came with it was too heavy for followers to appreciate.
Case studies were made of the lonely Old Testament
prophet. While this may be true for some of the prophets
in their vocation, to say that leaders today therefore
need to accept loneliness as part of leadership may be
overstating it. I believe leadership today has more to do
with team leadership.

Whether or not you are leading a small or a large
team of locals and/or internationals, team leadership is
far more effective than going it alone. Opponents to
this concept will have New Testament team leadership
models to reckon with – like our Lord as part of the
Trinity, with his 12 disciples and an inner core of Peter,
James and John; the disciples who formed the
Jerusalem leadership council; Paul and Barnabas, then
later Paul and Silas, and their doctor companion, Luke.
On the contrary, a 'lone ranger' today raises all kinds of
questions – like why are they not working with other
leaders; are they under authority; what about accountability; where does their counsel come from or do they
think they have cornered the market on God's wisdom?

Team leadership is biblical, sensible and practical.
Common sense dictates that sharing the load is far better than carrying it alone. Blessing shared is blessing
doubled; pressure shared is pressure halved. We must
recognise the tremendous pool of talented and gifted
men and women in the kingdom of God ready and waiting to be used for his glory. In what I am doing, I would
be foolish not to have a team of leaders working with
me. For not sharing the load, I would be brought to task
by those to whom I am responsible. As an ethos in the

movement, OM recognises the strength and advantages of team leadership over against the lone leader.

## Seeking counsel and mentoring

One protection in leadership is the godly counsel from others. As for myself, I have a small group of at least two other persons I can look to in dealing with any one issue or situation. Because issues and situations vary, I would seek counsel and advice from people who are knowledgeable and know the issues well. In addition, there is an informal (small) group of men I look to who can speak into my personal situation. It does not mean I am bugging them with questions every week, but it does mean I have an informal accountability arrangement with them. I have given them the freedom to ask me hard questions concerning my personal walk with the Lord, my marriage and family, and they are free at any time to speak into my situation.

We often think of seeking counsel from either our peers or from those who are our seniors. Sometimes, I like to seek counsel from children. I often find their answers refreshingly simple and relevant. If you think as a leader you cannot learn from children, then you are wiser than the Lord Jesus – who told his disciples to learn from them! I have often watched how adults lead and handle children. We adults assume children today will sing exactly the same songs we sang as kids (30 years ago); worst, we assume teens today will sing exactly the same songs we sang as teens (25 years ago). This is big mistake! This is an insult to them. Why not ask what they like to sing and do, for once? You will be surprised to discover that their taste and their level of understanding are more mature and advanced than you think.

Mentoring, or coaching, is discussed often in leadership. Some say leaders should take the opportunity to mentor younger people, while others encourage leaders to be mentored by others – or do both. One time, meeting as a group of leaders of OM, we asked ourselves how each of us was mentored, and by whom. To summarise, we discovered there was no one set way of mentoring, especially in a multi-cultural group, and that mentoring was different in various stages of our lives. As to the question by whom we were mentored, the answers were as varied as they were refreshingly enlightening. One or two said they were mentored by their godly father and/or mother; most of us named familiar names of leaders who had gone before us; one said a Muslim school teacher left an indelible mark on his life; famous Christian leaders whose ministry we had sat under had also mentored us; most of us could claim that books played a major part in our lives; almost all felt some degree of mentoring amongst ourselves. But the most enlightening revelation was to discover that we were all effectively mentored by our respective wives! In hindsight, I would have mentioned my children – I believe they have mentored me as a father and as a leader more than they realise.

## Bridging generational and cultural gaps

To be a leader today is more challenging than in the recent past. With globalisation and the shrinking of the earth – in terms of quick and easy travel – leadership has to reckon with a whole lot of issues not known in the past. It is easy to take sides. And as leaders, it is easy to show favouritism towards those we like and know. The tendency is to side with one generation against another

– usually the older against the younger, or vice versa. In an inter-denominational, multi-cultural ministry like OM, care is all the more needed that we do not give the appearance of favouritism.

The church is bigger than we think. God's work is far greater than we imagine. If your church is happily living in its own little world without the realisation that it is a part (however minute) of a whole, and that as believers, they are inextricably linked to believers of other lands and races, then they are missing out on the grand and majestic plan and purpose of God. And as leaders, you are missing the big picture God is trying to show you.

'Rejoice with those who rejoice and weep with those who weep' (Rom. 12:15, NASB) has far-reaching effects other than our little church, denomination or race ghetto. The church of God spreads far and wide, beyond any racial or national boundaries. They may slow it down, but no political boundaries can halt the advance of the church of God. There has been a sudden rise of nationalism – just watch the soccer World Cup to see my point. Christians dance to the tune of nationalism at the expense of their heavenly citizenship. Finding the balance will be a challenge.

As leaders of today, we will need to bridge generations, cultures and races. This task seems daunting, but it is not if taken at bite-size. Do whatever you can to link with others in God's worldwide family. Partner with them in the work of the gospel and in the task of world evangelism. I have seen many leaders playing such a role and I like what I have seen. Like me, I trust you will also attempt to do what you can in bridging the gaps for the sake of Jesus Christ.

Welcome to God's school of leadership!

# PART TWO

*Going, going . . .*

# Chapter Six

# Welcome to missions

Jesus . . . said . . . 'go . . . '

(Mt. 28:19, NIV)

*(Note: A word of explanation about terms. The word 'missions' refers to the total and complete enterprise of fulfilling the Great Commission. In this sense it is a comprehensive word. The word 'mission' (without the 's') refers to a specific purpose or goal to be undertaken say by a church or an organisation. It is not a grammatical oversight when you see the word 'missions' the way it's being used in this, and other books on the same subject.)*

Missions is not an option.

The command from Jesus to 'go' has mobilised a great army of dedicated Christians into missions through the centuries. And it still does. In a country where the word of the king is law, the only response from all his subjects is submission. Likewise, when Jesus the King tells us to go, we obey. Assuming that you are well on your way to becoming a genuine follower of Jesus, you will no doubt want to obey all that he taught.

If only it was that simple and straightforward! Unfortunately, missions is a lot more complex and complicated in this modern age among affluent, complex and knowledgeable Christians than it used to be, say fifty or so years ago. Before, missions was from the west to the rest; from the Northern to the Southern hemisphere. Now, church and missions growth are taking place at a pace far quicker in the east and the Southern hemisphere. Missions has to reckon with this phenomenon as it has a far-reaching impact in the overall balance in world missions.

If you are reading the same Bible as I am reading, you will notice that we do not have the privilege to pick and choose whether we want missions. If you are a Christian, you are in! Christianity is incomplete without an emphasis on missions. Let me use an illustration from Bagus, my Indonesian colleague. It is like following 9 out of the 10 steps in making a cup of coffee – you have the hot water, the mug, you add the sugar, cream, nice spoon to stir with, so on and so forth. But you miss the most important ingredient – coffee. In the end, you are drinking some liquid but it is not coffee. Missions (Parts Two and Three of this book) is essential to the Christian life (Part One) just as coffee is to making a cup of coffee.

Granted, 99 per cent of Christians will not end up as missionaries, but this fact does not release us from the responsibility.

But what is missions? How can I get started in it? What is my role? What about my obligation to my church and family? What about my job and career? These are real questions and they deserve proper answers. In the next chapters, you will learn in detail the practical import of the missions endeavour and your personal involvement.

I would like to begin in this chapter by offering 11 practical steps to help you navigate your way through missions.

## Step No. 1
## Find out what God is saying to you

There are many clear passages in the Bible where the mandate for missions is given. It is pretty clear what God wants all of us to do. What is unclear are the specifics. Paul could be specific in his mission to the Gentiles, just like Peter was to the Jews. You will need to determine specifically what God is saying to you about your role. We are all uniquely different. We are not clones. God works differently in each one of us. And God will lead us and show us differently.

To one he may be saying – go to another country; to another, it may be to a people group still unreached with the gospel. To one, he may say – be a church-planter; to another, be a Bible-translator. If you are serious about your role, ask him. The Holy Spirit is always at work, leading and guiding. It is hard to escape his influence especially when you want to know and want to play your part.

Besides prayer and meditating on God's word, it is important to keep abreast of what is happening around the world. God often uses information and news to stir us and spur us into action. And if all this leaves you befuddled, talk to your pastor or to some mature Christian leaders. They are generally wise and discerning. Better still, talk to missionaries, but be warned, they are naturally biased!

## Step No. 2
## Find out what your church is doing for missions

If your church is part of a main denomination, chances that it will have a missions committee, missions policy and missions programmes are high. I encourage you to consult with the chairperson or committee members. Missions committees are usually proactive about missions and always on the lookout for members who show an interest in getting involved. The more established churches generally have more established missions committees and programmes. Advice can be readily given. They may also have adopted some programmes, or projects, or have established a course for you to take that will get you eventually to the mission field. They will likely have enough resources to keep you there too. If you are from such a church, thank God!

If your church is an independent church, not too big, and still getting established, the chances of their sending you are not too bad, but not as good as the above. The degree of health of missions in such churches varies – from very active to completely inactive. If a church is continually plagued with leadership problems, relationship conflicts, financial lack, it is not impossible, but you had better be ready for some long hard work if you are serious about getting them to send you into missions.

Most churches are happy to help you work through your involvement in missions. They may have some denominational or church missions they want you to be involved in, but they may also be open for you to work with a mission agency in another country that the Lord has laid upon your heart. This kingdom (broad) mentality, rather than empire (narrow) mentality, is commendable.

If you are from a mega church, chances are they will have missions ministries that they will want to channel you into. They are big enough to do it on their own. If they are supportive of you joining another ministry, you have every reason to be glad.

**Step No. 3**
**Find out where your real interest lies**

Gone are the days of missions when missionaries would up and go, preach to the natives, never to return home, die and get buried in the field.

Approaches to missions have developed in the past several decades and have inevitably widened the scope and broadened the base of involvement. Globalisation has a profound impact on the nature of missions. Team effort (in contrast to the solo pioneer) is another positive development. The necessity of effective and adequate administration demands an ever-increasing need of multi-skilled personnel and staff. The advance of technology has given rise to the demand for a whole new communication- and computer-savvy generation of missionaries.

What does it mean for you? Plenty. For one, there is never any unemployment, and certainly no such thing as full employment in missions. Every agency I know is understaffed. Vacancies are sometimes left unfilled for months and years simply because there is not enough talent to go round. Bernd Gulker, the General Director of the two OM ships, told me that it is common knowledge in the merchant navy world that there is a dire shortage of marine engineers. Seldom on both the ships have we ever enjoyed a full complement of marine engineers, or deck officers for that matter. If the merchant navy world, with all its finances and benefits, cannot attract mariners, just imagine how difficult it is to find God-fearing, missions-loving seafarers ready to pitch in to sail on our ships without the usual salary and overseas allowance.

In reality, this is good news for you. If you have some basic skills, it will not be difficult to fit you in. If you have a relevant skill, perfect. Let me give you some inside information – the two premium skills most needed and in great demand that will land you a job in missions faster than you can blink your eyes (I am exaggerating) are – accounting and IT! Agencies are desperate for people with such skills. Medical personnel are at a premium but this is more specialised. Accounting and IT are more essential – we all need bean-counters, geeks and nerds!

## Step No. 4
## Find out what mission agencies are doing

There are literally hundreds, if not thousands of agencies that God has raised up and Christians have initiated. This is exciting.

You may get the occasional bad press about Christian organisations, mission agencies and Christian leaders. But don't let it stop you from believing in the best of the majority of Christian enterprises that are doing a good job. One bad egg should not mar the credibility of the whole basket.

Mission agencies are all unique. The more established ones are more so, in that they have stood the ravage of time and the onslaught of good and bad human history. They are unique because the founders or initiators all believed God had prompted them to act and had shown them the way to go. That does not mean agencies exist in perpetuity – even good ones have ceased operating. The fact that many still remain in vibrancy proves their enduring qualities and relevance. Seeing people saved by Jesus is never going to go out of fashion!

Mission agencies may have some degree of overlap in their ministries, but their emphases differ. You have agencies and organisations that concentrate on student work. Student work can be further divided into categories – such as secondary, tertiary, graduate, foreign or international. There are agencies specialising in Bible translation, literacy, publication and distribution work, relief and development, education and training. Medical work is extensive around the world – only God knows what tremendous change they have brought into the world at large. Just think of the leprosy work and the meaning this has brought to people inflicted with the disease. You will also find agencies in pioneering and church-planting work – this kind of work is usually done in places where there is hardly any Christian witness. It calls for a different type of missionary. And don't forget the agencies that use ships and planes to spread the gospel and to do good in general!

Marvel at the choices found in the missions enterprise. It is overwhelming, but don't let it stop you from finding out which ones capture your interest and imagination. You may have real difficulty deciding on one but be assured you are not alone. Remember to talk to others and find out all you can. Pastors and mission leaders will be more than happy to answer your questions. Find out too about the requirements to join an agency. Membership has its privileges, and its responsibilities. But you know this already!

## Step No. 5
## Try out with a visit or go on a mission trip

I have different advice for people who want to get involved in missions. For a person who is thinking about a longer period of several years or a life time of involvement, I suggest a visit to the place or people or ministries first. This is particularly helpful in the process of making a final decision. Many issues and questions can be sorted out on such a visit. Expectations, work conditions, local customs and culture, rules and regulations, education facilities for those with children, field care, safety and evacuation (more relevant than ever!), budgetary concerns, transport, health care, job opportunities, are just some of the questions a person needs to find answers to. If the answers to your questions are unsatisfactory (remember there is no perfect place on earth), at least you are making the decision with your eyes wide open. And if you finally decide not to go (and you will feel bad) at least it is an informed, and I trust, an intelligent decision.

For people who are not sure if missions is their cup of tea, I believe a short mission trip is a help in determining what cup of tea they really like. Go on a mission trip. Find out firsthand what it is like to be involved in missions. Never mind if it is to a place you have visited as a tourist. There is no rule that says you can't do some touristy things on a mission trip either. But you will get to learn the dynamics of missionary life. Most short term trippers get some of the basic issues of life sorted out, and this alone is worth the trip. Others may come to the conclusion that missions is 'not for me – I just can't stand the food, the dirt, the . . .' For such people, mission agencies are only too happy that they remain at home and just send the money! Most short trippers have a positive experience. 'We love it!' seems to be a common feeling after a trip. A positive experience can still be had even when things go wrong. Most trips and teams tend to have problems anyway and who says we can't learn positive things from bad situations? Thankfully, as I have said, the feedback is overwhelmingly positive for short trippers.

My recommendation – sign up on one of your church mission trips, or if there are none, mission agencies will be more than willing to help.

**Step No. 6**
**Find your match**

Sounds like a marriage. The principle may not be too different. You need to know if you will be happy working with the mission agency or ministry you have decided to join. If you feel happiness has nothing to do with it, fine. Then be miserable. I don't see anything wrong with a good and happy match between the individual and the agency. I would even go to the extent of saying that if you are not happy with the mission agency, do not join it. It is plain common sense.

By this time, you will already have an idea or a preference as to what you want to do, where you want to go and what agency or ministry you want to join. You will have discovered that there are agencies specialising in geographical areas - like Europe, North, Sub-Sahara and Southern Africa, Middle East and Central Asia, South Asia, East Asia, the Pacific, North America, Central and Latin America (I am not sure if there is a mission to the Arctic and the Antarctic!) or in religious blocs of the world. When you have such knowledge and information, you can start narrowing down the choices.

It is important now for you to find out the organisation's culture, purpose, goals, ethos, policies, practices, and commitment to its members. Ideally, it is wise to join one that has an office in your country that can provide you with the communication, support and back-up. Where there is none, an agency will usually have a representative, a committee, or another agency representing them.

Mission work comes in all types. In addition, all sorts of jobs and functions are also available. There are field workers, evangelists, ministry workers, and there are those working behind the scenes – like the bookkeepers, accountants, secretaries, personnel staff, administrators, counsellors and hospitality staff. What do you see yourself doing?

It is also important to know your gifting. One indication of your gifting is whether or not you enjoy what you are doing. Some people are relational; they love meeting people. If you are one of these, working behind the scenes may not be a good idea, unless in your behind-the-scenes work you have found an outlet for meeting people and building relationships with them. In missions, people think only when you are out winning people to Christ that you are doing real work, and sitting in the office is not serious missions. This dichotomy is unnecessary. Unfortunately, I often come across people gifted in administration trying so hard to be church planters and ministry people placed in desk jobs. Both end up frustrated and unfruitful.

Give yourself time to find a good match. It does not have to be a perfect match. And finding that out is best done on the field, in practice, not just in our armchair at home.

## Step No. 7
## Decide on duration of commitment

Short-term or long-term? Long-term or life-long term? This is an important issue for prospective missionaries.

The duration, as important as it is, is not as crucial as the commitment. A person may be involved in missions for a long time, but there can be a lack of commitment.

Commitment is a quality that should permeate into all aspects of our life, including missions. A person may not be long in the mission field, or may have never been in a mission field, but this person can be totally sold out and committed to missions. This, I believe, is an important distinction.

I have read articles negating short-term missions. Writers of such articles lament and question their usefulness. Derogatory terms are used to describe, or slander, such efforts. One big-name missionary statesman and author of many books did this at a gathering of Christian leaders that I attended. He effectively reduced and demeaned the work of God in agencies specialising in short-term missions in his hour-long speech. Later, I wrote to him to let him know that what he did was discourteous, ungentlemanly and damaging to those who were involved in short-term missions. Sadly, instead of apologising, he further reduced short-term ministries by calling it 'parasitic'. I was disappointed.

One needs to understand that work like Youth With a Mission, OM and many similar ministries specialise in short-term missions in view of long-term work. This missionary statesman did not appreciate that many of these ministries are anchored by hard working, diligent long-termers who believe with all their heart and soul that God can use someone genuinely fired up in short-term missions. Short-term missions can dovetail perfectly with long-term work. OM does it all the time. What people do not know is that many short-termers make a comeback as long-termers. I am one. And I wholeheartedly endorse both short-term and long-term missions.

In the past, say a century or half ago, missionaries went for life – defined as long-term. These days, the average long-termer lasts between 10-15 years of service. There are exceptions, but the rule is that families do not last as long as they would like. Their children grow up and their continuing education is a major concern. Where should they be educated? If you were in the middle of the Sahara, where would you send them? The nearest MK (Missionary Kid) school is in another country, and it does not offer Mandarin or Japanese as a language option. What do you do? Many parents make the hard decision to head for home. The importance of an efficient home office and their request for help makes the return less guilt-ridden and more positive. From home, they continue to be committed to missions, raising awareness, challenging people to pray, raising funds and recruiting others to take over the positions they have vacated.

Short-term or long-term? My suggestion is, try short-term – for a year or two, for a start. Then you are in a better position to gauge your long-term durability. Whether short or long-term, I pray you are committed to missions for life!

## Step No. 8
## Do your homework

Missions is teamwork. In Romans 10:14, Paul pleaded with readers to send preachers. In missions, we tend to glorify the preacher - i.e. the goer. We make light work of those who do not go into missions. In the past few years, books urging Christians to be senders are addressing this imbalance. As you go into missions, it is important that you esteem the senders. They are not second class. They are as much a part of missions as those in the frontline.

Who are the senders and what can they do that is crucial to the missions enterprise?

Senders are your church, your church members, friends, family, missions committee, donors, prayer partners and anyone else who has an interest in standing behind you. Two very key relationships you must be aware of and consciously seek to build are with your pastor and the chairperson of the missions committee. If you do not like them, then you had better learn to if you want to be a missionary. If you don't win them over, you are going to have a hard time. If you learn to cultivate your relationship with them, you stand only to benefit. Seek their advice, listen to them, say hello to their spouses, pat their dog, tickle their cat, just do it for Jesus and for missions. In return, you get their support, and when you get their support, you also get the church's support. This support is crucial. It will either make or break your missionary career.

Church support comes in the form of prayer. Begin by attending the church prayer meeting. Learn to share your concern. It takes humility to ask for prayer. Do you pray for the needs of others? Do you even ask what their needs are? When members pray, the Lord will lay upon their hearts the burden. That's where financial support comes. I have known of missionaries returning home because they have not done their homework in raising financial support. And the reason for this failure is that they have lost touch with their senders. God will supply all our needs if he has called, right? And you will find that God uses his people most of the time to meet your needs. Develop your people skills. Build relationships. Maintain them with emails, phone calls, visits, gifts, cards, or whatever it takes.

When the church cares enough for you, they will pray. When they pray, they will give. When this takes place, you are adequately supported and prayed for so that you do not have to worry about your next meal on the field, and that leaves you to concentrate on getting the job done. When you do your homework, you will benefit in return.

There is no short cut to this even when you have arrived at your destination. This is long-term work.

## Step No. 9
## Preparation

Preparation is half the battle won. But what sort of preparation is needed for missions? Is it possible to under-prepare, or over-prepare? Yes, it is possible to under- or over- prepare. But then, what sort of preparation is enough?

I tend to think people going on short (two week) mission trips generally over-prepare. Some churches spend months preparing a few people for a four day trip. They get trippers to go through courses, learn skills, read up, write up messages, research and so on. Generally speaking, there is over-preparation. I heard of a student team where the leader prepared many messages to preach but discovered on arrival that much of what he prepared had no relevance. Better to prepare teams to be flexible and ready for any contingency. Some basic communication skills and orientation are advantageous. Many churches have done a good job teaching and training members. Members are more trained and more prepared than they realise.

More preparation is needed if you are thinking in terms of several years. Some preparation can be done before leaving and the rest can be done when you arrive. Additional training can be in the form of refresher courses and formal study.

Before departure, the mission agencies will probably want you to attend their orientation course. You will be briefed on the corporate culture of the agency, its values, some cross-cultural communication tips, travel, visa application, security and so on. The longer you sign up for, the longer the preparation course will be.

Upon arrival, you will go through another period of adaptation. You will need to learn how the team operates, group dynamics, teamwork, your role and responsibility, maintaining your spiritual edge and the local culture. There will also be time set aside for language acquisition. The first few months will be like a honeymoon. After that, routine sets in and you may get frustrated over the lack of progress in your language acquisition. You still cannot communicate with the locals and you cannot even get around without an interpreter. At this stage, perseverance is needed. All missionaries get over this phase and become effective communicators.

Further education may be needed after several years. Even the best missionary gets tired. Taking some time away from the ministry – be it for study, for rest or for refreshment, can do a world of good to your overall well-being. This is a good time to upgrade some skills, catch up with friends and supporters, deepen your understanding of your ministry by learning from others who have written much about it, or pursue that theological degree that you have always wanted.

## Step No. 10
## Honouring our parents

Honouring our parents is a biblical injunction. Different cultures honour their parents in different ways. Generally Asian cultures, like the Japanese, Korean, Thai, Indonesian and Chinese revere their parents. As our parents grow older, our father becomes the patriarch of the clan. When the patriarch passes on, the matriarch replaces him. It is not unusual to find Asian children (grown-ups) flying from all over the world just to get back in time to celebrate occasions like their parents' auspicious sixtieth, seventieth or eightieth birthday or the reunion dinner on Lunar New Year's eve. When there is a death, the same happens.

In missions, parental consent for the would-be missionary is a critical aspect of our obedience. Obedience to God inevitably collides head on with our parents' wishes. For reasons unknown, Asian parents seem to have a low regard for Christian work and Christian workers. Somehow there is an assumption that the church is the worst paymaster – pastors are such poor people (perhaps they think pastors are the Christian version of the austere Buddhist monk!). Non-Christian parents are basically clueless about missions and if you tell them you want to be a missionary, they will assume you are joining the ranks of the Christian monks. It is therefore not unusual to face parental objection in this area.

Several years back, when a young lady wanted to join OM, her mother threatened to burn down the church! Thankfully it was only a verbal threat. This was an extreme reaction but showed how real an issue like this is for an Asian. We prayed, and thankfully, within a week or so, the mother had a change of heart. She was even at the airport to send off her daughter!

Another set of parents are those who did not fulfil their missions vow earlier in life. They had heard God's call. They had even stood up at a missions rally to make the commitment to go into all the world, but they had not gone. Instead, career concerns had crowded out obedience to God. Now, they have come full circle. Their children have grown up. Perhaps, they think, God can use their children where once they themselves had failed. They are volunteering their children! In some cases, children make their decision to be involved independently. In other cases, they simply have no interest at all. It is the parents who are pushing. These days, when we receive requests from parents offering their children for service, we ask them to get their children to contact us personally. We want to hear it from them, not from their parents!

The most disappointing set of parents I have come across are Christian parents who refuse to allow their son or daughter to join missions. They attend church, listen to missions speakers, they may even contribute financially, but they will not permit their own children to go. Let others go instead, but not theirs. Recently, my own children asked if they could sail on the MV Doulos. I assured them that nothing would please me more than their desire to serve the Lord. Granted they are still young, but I want them to hear from their parents that serving God this way has all our blessings. Of course, when the time comes, they will have to work through issues with the church about their intentions and so on. But they know they have our affirmation. Once I asked Justin if he was embarrassed about his father being a missionary. 'No,' he said, 'on the contrary, I am very proud!' My heart leapt just to hear it from him.

Honouring your parents means you may have to postpone your departure. Often unspoken is their fear of losing you. Assurances from you and the church will go a long way. Another real fear is the loss of income when you are gone. They are afraid that in your absence, they will suffer financially, especially if you have been contributing to their upkeep all along. Some churches I know have a mission policy that provides for the parents – it may not be market rate, but what is important is the thought behind it. Such a token of care and love for the missionary's parents is a great testimony to them. The church missions committee can also arrange regular visits to your aged parents, which is another winner.

## Step No.11
## Now that you have arrived

You finally make it to your destination. Well done. It is the beginning, but a good beginning.

By now, you would have a supportive church, sympathetic family and friends standing behind you. You are with a mission agency you are happy with. You are getting to know the team members and their peculiarities. You are beginning to get a feel of the real place and people whom you have been preparing to meet for so long. Let me introduce you now to the various identities as a missionary.

You would have realised by now the term 'missionary' is forbidden. Sorry, I should have told you earlier. In reality, the mission agency would have briefed you way in advance. Except for some 'Christian' countries, many countries in the world do not welcome religious workers. They welcome and provide visas for professionals and business people who can provide jobs and training for their people. Bona fide students wanting to learn their language and customs are usually welcomed also.

Missions have developed along such lines in the past two decades – instead of going in strictly as a missionary, creative ways have been used to gain entry. This is not unlike what Paul did as a tent-maker to support his ministry. The term 'tent-maker' has been developed and used to describe missionaries who support themselves with some sort of work in order to provide for and facilitate their ministry. The word 'tent-making' is used particularly in restricted access countries. Often new tent-makers wrestle with this concept and experience tension over the dual role. Some feel it is like playing Dr Jekyll and Mr Hyde. The issue of integrity, honesty and transparency complicates matters. You can read books to help you see the validity of tent-making, but it is of little help when you are living in a real situation with real risk. Having said this, I am pleased to inform you that there are many successful tent-makers in missions today. I believe the quality that distinguishes them is their ability to be flexible and accepting of ambiguity.

Tent-makers come in various forms. One can be a student of the host language – this normally has a lifespan of several years, as one is only allowed that length of time to learn a language. But then, I have come across people who are professional students! Teaching is also a great opportunity. Many countries are opening up to teachers of the English language. Some are quite particular and they demand native English speakers while others are not so fussy. Another platform is the professional. I know of a man who is a consultant representing a business although he has very little trading to show for it. I also know of another man who is a tour agent in his tent-making role. There will always be the tension to know how much time and effort to divide between work and ministry. Then again, this tension is there even if you remain at home holding a regular job and actively involved in church!

Missions today has a whole new spectrum of opportunities for the lay missionary never before available. Don't dismiss yourself if you don't think you can be a traditional missionary. There is no limit to the possibilities. Credit yourself with some resourcefulness and imagination. The Lord can use you.

Let me close this practical chapter with this question you may have asked yourself: 'What if after reading this chapter, I am still not convinced about getting involved?'

I accept that the majority of Christians will not become missionaries. This pattern is historical. The majority of Christians will remain at home. I do not and will not judge you. Feeling better?

However, let me reiterate – whether remaining at home or going, missions is not an option.

If you are not going, then you must make every effort to be a sender. Books have been written about being a sender. In a nutshell, a sender gives, supports, prays and does a host of things to make it possible for goers to go and to facilitate their effectiveness when they are there. A sender's role can be more demanding than a goer's. Chapter Eleven will give you practical tips on involvement as a sender.

Senders are part of the team. Make sure you are an active team member!

# Chapter Seven

# The twenty-first century missionary

What does the twenty-first century missionary look like?

I have often been asked to speak on twenty-first century missions. I suppose churches who invite me to speak on this subject are either curious about whether there can be a marriage between the twenty-first century (the new now) and missions (the old then), or they are just giving a catchy title to a tired subject.

Viv Thomas, a fellow writer and a good friend, once said something about change that I will always remember. Change is inevitable – but you probably know that. But some still think we have an option to choose not to change. Viv said, 'we have no choice but to change.'

All of us are creatures of habit and of comfort. Change disrupts our comfortable and sometimes sinful habits. For some of us who are older and in leadership position, we must change, or we become irrelevant. A lot of effort is spent fighting it. Of course not all things ought to change, but if change means better facilitation of workers into missions, improved methods, greater people care and wider spread of the gospel, then change we must!

Some things in missions will remain the same, but many things have changed. Let me run through some of the changes I see.

## Speed in communication

What had taken all of six months to communicate a century or even several decades ago, now takes seconds! While visiting a friend in Lhasa, Tibet, I could not resist the temptation to call home to Singapore. I was instantly connected to my family. We live in the days of instant communication. Remember the moment Ronaldo kicked the ball to score the second goal at the 2002 World Cup Final in Japan? Half way across the world, Brazilians shouted 'Goooaaaal!!!' just as the ball crashed into the net. That's instantaneous transmission.

## Ease of travel

Just slightly behind electronic and satellite communication is the ease and convenience of modern day travel. Nineteenth century missionaries to China and the Far East took months to get here on steamships. Today, almost all major Asian and European airlines have direct non-stop flights back and forth every day. It only takes an average of 13 hours to fly from east to west, and a shorter 12 hours west to east. Read a few chapters of a book, watch two movies and gulp down two airplane meals and you have arrived. If you fly from Asia eastward to North America, you actually arrive on the same day, and perhaps the same hour. It's almost surreal. The world is getting smaller (it isn't really but travel by air gives you this impression).

## Modern day terrorism

Terrorism, in its broadest application, is as old as humankind. But after 11 September 2001, it took a sinister turn – in that people do not feel safe anywhere any more. Now, people believe terror can happen anywhere to anyone. Terrorism, coupled with religious militancy, the increase in illegal immigration and the refugee problem, has changed the face of missions altogether. Entrance into traditionally welcoming countries is getting harder.

Yet, God is working like never before. At best, we can only catch up with what he is doing in the hearts of people, especially in countries and among people devastated and destroyed by conflicts caused by humanity. Every day there are heart-warming stories of men and women, boys and girls, young and old, saved in the knowledge of Christ.

I can go on writing about twenty-first century missions, about the more biblical and holistic approach in ministering to hurting Aids victims and the poor; about the new missions micro-entrepreneurs who use their entrepreneurial skills to bring about a significant difference in the lives of ordinary people struggling to make a living; about the children, teens, youths, young adults doing their small bit so that others may hear the good news; about the key role churches are playing in reaching unreached groups, and about the blossoming of what I call comprehensive missions – the engagement of all kinds of people for all kinds of roles in all types of time duration. Indeed we have more reasons to be engaged in missions in the twenty-first century than at any time in the past.

Having said that, does it mean we can all go now? If only this was possible and true – the world would be reached with the gospel several times over!

The key to successful missions in the third millennium is still people. Leonard Ravenhill said that while we are looking for better methods, God is looking for better men (and women, of course). God's method is still a Man – his incarnate Son – who came to live and die among us so that we may follow his example. God's method is still in his people – who will, like his Son, incarnate the gospel among peoples who have yet to hear and respond.

So what kind of people are we talking about? Are we looking for the same kind of people that we used to have half a century or so back? In the context of today, are the qualities of yesteryears still valid?

I am going to suggest a list of ten qualities needed in order to be a twenty-first century missionary. I am aware the word 'missionary' is the last word one should use to describe one's vocation especially when living and working in a restrictive country. I use it here because I believe it essentially describes a noble vocation, before the negative connotations became attached to this word. These qualities are not set in concrete, nor are they in order of significance. They may even reinforce the same qualities descriptive of past missionaries. See if I am describing you.

## Conviction

Perhaps this comes as no surprise to people who are familiar with missions and have read enough old missionary biographies. This was the obvious and unmistakable trait of missionaries in the past. I believe conviction is not only valid for today; it is fundamental. Today's missionaries-to-be who are short of conviction in their Christian beliefs and in their missions compulsion ought to cultivate this trait.

Conviction means one is convinced about something. Different people possess different convictions. On a phone-in radio programme in New Zealand, one lady called in to the host to express in no uncertain terms that she was absolutely convinced that guinea pigs had rights. I supposed at two in the morning, people tend to say things out of the ordinary. George Booth, the director of OMNZ, told me about the man who phoned in to propose his theory that the world was inverted – meaning, we're all living inside the globe. This theory proved to this man why people did not fall off the earth and satisfactorily explained away the law of gravity. People do have screwy convictions.

In missions, there are some things you must be convinced of. Firstly, you must be convinced that men are lost without Christ. 'For there is one God and one mediator between God and men, the man Jesus Christ.' (1 Tim. 2:5, NIV) There is salvation in no other. In the age of religious tolerance, the uniqueness of Christ's life, death and resurrection can easily be lost. The cry for universalism – that everyone will be saved, and that all religions lead to God so it doesn't matter which one you believe in, is all too attractive. Salvation comes only when one believes and calls on the name of the Lord.

Secondly, one needs to be convinced of the reality of hell and eternal punishment. I believe this knowledge alone was the motivation for many in the past to get involved in missions. This is a difficult subject especially when we try to balance God's love with his justice. This is also a painful conviction to hold because it affects all of us as it is closer to home – where we know of close friends, relatives and even family members who are living without the knowledge of eternal deliverance.

While speaking in a church, I noticed a young boy seated in the back row, crying uncontrollably. Later, I learned that his anguish was because of the sudden real-isation that some of his friends in his class did not know Jesus and therefore were headed for hell. How does one counsel an anguished boy over such a devastating truth? It's not easy. I pacified him by reminding him that he would also see some of his friends in heaven. I sug-gested to him to pray faithfully for his friends.

This leads me to the last conviction – the reality of heaven. This conviction is a strong motivation to keep us engaged in missions.

There are other convictions one can develop, but I sus-pect the three convictions above are more than enough. Old fashioned or not, conviction is important.


## Commitment

We find in the Bible that God is a God of commitment. He is committed to his word, his people, his church, his purpose. Everything.

And he expects no less from us. Commitment is a quality that is a close cousin to faithfulness, reliability, dependability and trustworthiness. It is a good and desirable quality.

The first and greatest commandment calls for total commitment: 'Love the Lord your God with *all* your heart and with *all* your soul and with *all* your mind.' (Mt. 22:37, NIV – emphasis mine). A pastor prayed to the Lord the following: 'Lord, I want you to be first in my life; my ministry, second; my family, third, and self, last.' This was his expression of commitment to the Lord. Then he heard a small voice saying to him, 'I don't want to be first.' The pastor was puzzled. 'Why not, Lord?' The voice replied, 'I want to be ALL.' He wants our all, not just to be first.

We also learn in Scripture that God's character demands a response. That means if God is holy, he expects us to be holy: 'Be holy, because I am holy.' (1 Pet 1:16, NIV) If he is righteous, he expects us to be clothed with righteousness, and if he is faithful, he expects us to be the same. He is looking for people of commitment who are faithful to what they are committed to.

People tend to blame God when bad things happen, but they don't credit God when good things happen! *Commitment is a virtue especially when things go wrong.*

For every success story, there are probably many unsuccessful ones. One of the funniest books I have read is entitled *101 Useless Japanese Inventions*. The funniest invention must be the hat with a roll of toilet paper mounted on top for people who have the flu and need to blow their nose on the run. Who would want to be seen wearing such a hat! It was obviously a failed product, but one cannot fault the inventor for lacking in imagination; wisdom perhaps, but not imagination. In missions, success is different because the value system is different. What we term success may not be so in God's eyes and what we think is failure may well be the complete opposite. By human standards, the Lord Jesus would have been termed a failure – at the end of his earthly life, he could not boast of any earthly accomplishments. Even his disciples and friends abandoned him. The world would term that a failure.

We have the tendency to be half-hearted in our commitment. Things are done without conviction. Work is done halfway; duty is discharged with little enthusiasm. We play it safe; getting involved only when plans go well. As soon as there is a chance of failure, we are quick to disassociate ourselves.

So much of life needs commitment. Imagine making your marriage vows with only 80 per cent commitment –

20 per cent is too high for any marriage to go wrong. The same is true with work, career, being parents and so on.

## Resolve

While commitment has to do with obligation, dedication and heartfelt action, the quality of 'resolve' (or resolute) has an added value to it. In one dictionary 'resolve' implies making a firm mental decision or intention. It means dogged determination; a never-give-up and never-say-die attitude.

There is a cartoon picture of a frog being swallowed head first by a stork. Instead of resigning itself to impending doom, the frog makes a desperate attempt at strangling the stork's slim throat. The picture shows the stork's eyes popping out from suffocation. The caption below the cartoon says: 'Never, ever give up!' It perfectly depicts what I mean by resolve.

The apostle Paul said in Acts 20:24: 'I consider my life worth nothing to me, if only I may finish the race and complete the task the Lord Jesus has given me – the task of testifying to the gospel of God's grace.' (NIV) Paul was focused. He did not care about his life. All he cared about was finishing the race God set for him and to complete the task of spreading the gospel. Paul was resolute.

Being resolute means you are disciplined. Discipline involves cultivating godly habits and behaviour that will result in godly character. Discipline, alas, is made a lot harder in an age of plenty and of indulgence.

## Courage

The events of (and post) 9/11 have had a great impact in the course of missions. Immediately following 9/11, people were paralysed by fear. Missionaries and churches were no exceptions. I know of missionaries who upped and left the mission field on September 12 because of fear. Now, missions has to reckon with the element of fear.

Risk and danger are relative. What is safe for one may not be so for another. Statistics showing that there are more deaths on the roads than people killed by terrorist attacks in an average year will not make any difference in people's outlook. Fear is here to stay.

Come to think of it, nowhere is really safe. I believe the safest place is to be in the centre of God's will. You may think you are in the safest place in the world but this is a delusion. You can be doing your own thing and minding your own business and death can still visit you without notice. No one can boast about being in a safe place or about a safe tomorrow because no one can be absolutely sure. I live on the tiny island of Singapore and there is a tendency to think that it is a safe place. The best and safest bet is still to be in God's will. No one can guarantee safety and safety can be an illusion, if it is outside the presence and will of God.

I am dismayed by the lack of courage of my fellow countrymen and fellow Christians. '*Kiasee*' is a popular Hokkien (a Chinese dialect) expression transliterated 'afraid to die' in English. *Kiasee* accurately described the prevalent feelings then – when 9/11 took place, Singaporeans were so *kiasee* that they actually cancelled holiday trips to nearby Johor Baru and Malacca – two popular weekend destinations. It was quite ludicrous, but fear can lead people to do the ridiculous. Hundreds of schools also cancelled their annual field trips. There was a general paralysis.

Unfortunately, this had affected missions. It still does. Parents, families and churches are asking for assurance of safety when a family member volunteers to be a missionary. Most mission agencies have suffered a drop in recruits as a result.

Fear is natural for human beings. But as Christians, our response should be one of courage; facing it head on. Oswald Chambers wrote something insightful in his book *My utmost for his highest*.[2] He said that the average view of the Christian life is that there is deliverance from trouble. This is incorrect. It is deliverance in trouble – which is very different.

The Bible is filled with stories of people who were afraid, but God gave them courage. To Abraham – Genesis 15:1, Joshua in Joshua 8:1, Elijah – 2 Kings 1:15, Jeremiah in Jeremiah 1:8, Daniel in Daniel 10:12, Paul – Acts 18:9, John – Revelation 1:17, he said, 'do not be afraid'. Fear not. To his disciples he said in Luke 12:4, '. . . do not be afraid of those who kill the body and after that can do no more.' But fear God instead. Overcome our natural fear with a healthy fear of the Lord.

Right after 9/11, TS (not his real name), a colleague who works in Tajikistan, requested prayer for the team he was leading to investigate the refugee situation in Afghanistan. There were reports that people were dying not because of the bombing, but because of the famine. Crisis causes fear, but in this case, it gave TS and his team an opportunity. The team was able to confirm that the reports were true and this resulted in several truckloads of relief materials being sent to the 300,000 Afghan refugees. Today, there is an ongoing work among these refugees bordering Tajikistan. Courage is facing crisis head on.

I believe young people today are especially suited to taking risks. Just watch some of the X-treme sports pro-

---

[2] Oswald Chambers, *My utmost for His highest* (Barbour publishing Inc.), page – August 2

grammes on TV. They attempt stunts others cannot even dare imagine. Why can't Christian youths show the same courage in serving God?

## Compassion

While courage, resolve, conviction and commitment are steely, compassion brings balance with its tenderness. Compassion's cousin words are mercy, sympathy, pity, love and kindness.

When Jesus 'saw the crowds, he had compassion' (Mt. 9:36, NIV)

I would describe compassion as the kindly disposition and ministry for the relief of those who are suffering and in need.

Let me follow up with an incident after the team was able to send in truckloads of relief materials to the Afghan refugees before the onslaught of the harsh winter. At one of the camps, a team member wrote, 'On the first day of our distribution, we met a three-year-old orphan who lost both of his parents in the 1999 earthquake. On a cold, snowy day, this three-year-old stood patiently outside, barefooted. We fitted him with a brand new pair of boots.'

Another team spoke of Abdul who stood in tattered clothes telling about his five children, all of whom were sick. As a farmer, he had sold his land several years ago because of the severe drought. He had no means of earning an income. A proud man, Abdul cried as he told of his life in one of the poorest villages in the area.

What are your feelings having just read the two stories above? My heart is filled with compassion. We must remain sensitive towards those who are suffering. Over familiarity with suffering can cause one to be annoyed and angry. Pray this will never happen in your life.

## Communicative

The ability to communicate is another quality badly needed in twenty-first century missions.

No, I am not referring to the skill in which we use information technology, the computer, email, the Internet, or even SMS (texting). At a wedding dinner not long ago, I was seated next to a table of young professionals. The young men wore dark shirts with matching silvery ties and their hair gelled to the desired style, while the young women all wore dark dresses with their hair bleached semi-blonde or brown. I noticed they were all SMS'ing (the finger generation?) on their mobile phones throughout the evening's ten-course meal. What was odd was that they were hardly seen carrying on a conversation with those seated around the table! People are better at communicating with gadgets than with people. I am not talking about this kind of communication.

By communicative, I mean people communicating with people. Do not misunderstand, I am not against IT and computers. As a matter of fact, I cannot work without such tools. But at best they are only tools. They can never replace face-to-face and heart-to-heart communication.

By communicative, I also mean the ability to relate to people. This takes time and energy. Kamal, my Sudanese colleague, likes to chide us who are from developed countries by saying, 'You have the watch, but we have the time.' Building relationships is not and should not be time-bound; it should be done as in the cultures in the Middle East, North Africa, South and Central Asia. Workers in these regions spent a huge amount of time relating to locals through informal visits and friendship building. Drinking tea, they say, is a skill one must quickly learn. Surrounding this custom is the culture of sharing – of problems, of blessings, happiness and suffering. So if you want to be a missionary in some of these places, learn to listen and communicate, and learn to drink tea!

It is interesting to note in the four Gospels the number of occasions Jesus spent time with people in informal settings – at a wedding, at a funeral, in private homes, at celebrations, by the sea, on boats, up in the mountains and down in the valleys. He spent time talking to huge crowds and with families and individuals. He even prepared a seafood BBQ on the beach for his disciples!

We have to make time. We rush around the whole day doing things but at the end, we discover we have not gone anywhere any quicker. In many societies the common complaint is that there is not enough time. A watchmaker invented a watch that could read 25 hours a day. He simply took six seconds out of each minute and at the end of the day, there is a gain of an 'extra' hour. This watchmaker was ingenious, but you still end up with exactly 24 hours!

Learn to communicate. I have a confession to make. People who know me say I have a sense of humour. Humour diffuses tension and I often ask the Lord for spontaneity in my humour. But I was not like that earlier in life. For many years, I suffered from low self-esteem and shyness, especially towards the opposite sex. I remember in my teens, I happened to like one girl in another class in my school. In my shyness, I could never summon enough courage to make her acquaintance. Soon, my class knew that I liked her. Then her class came to know that I liked her. Eventually, she came to know about it. This went on for three years, until we were both in the same class. I would imagine walking up to her to say what had taken me days to rehearse but that never happened. I was too shy (a coward actually). I dared only to send her birthday, New Year and Christmas cards. But as soon as we were back in class, I was absolutely tongue-tied. Until we left school, I never plucked up enough courage to talk to her. She eventually married someone rich, I gathered. This was the price I paid for shyness (obviously the Lord is sovereign – I am happily married to Irene instead). As I recall this episode of my growing years, I wonder why I was so dumb!

It was only much later when I started serving the Lord that I became less bashful. When I was thrust into public speaking and singing before crowds, I fought tooth and nail against shyness. We were motivated to deny ourselves and be fools for Christ. So I thought, for Jesus, I would attempt things that I would not normally dare. Maybe you are like me. I pray that for Jesus' sake, you would overcome your shyness. Some women, like my wife Irene, are not very good speaking upfront. But that doesn't matter. Just call up some friends for high tea. This is often the most natural setting for women. Simply gossip the gospel – which, by the way, is a biblical practice!

## Creativity

A creative person is not logged on to one way of doing things. In the attempt to try new things, a creative person does not face dead ends. Dead ends are just an opportunity or challenge to show greater creativity. A creative person is not just preoccupied with doing things right, but is usually seen doing the right things.

Creative people are not perfectionists. Perfectionists are concerned about crossing the t's and dotting the i's. They are more interested in the details and often get lost in them. A creative person looks at the big picture and finds ways to do a better and more beautiful job.

A creative person also maintains some form of openness. The openness to accept, adapt and adopt other creative ideas. Some people think only the young are open to ideas, and the old are not. Sometimes the reverse is true. The lack of openness plagues both young and old. Their rigidity causes them to dig in to their views and be stubborn in their opinion. A closed mentality is unattractive. It will lose friends and influence.

More than ever, missions today is in need of creative people. With political, social, religious and economic uncertainties and instability in many countries, missionaries must remain adaptable.

Central Asia Development Agency is one such creative enterprise that is the brainchild of Dave and Pam. It is an NGO (non-government organisation) engaged in activities that will result in the improved living conditions and welfare of the people it works amongst. One project was to start an email hub in the country's capital. For this, 50 secondhand computers and hardware were collected and the container shipped to Tajikistan. It went via Russia, Mongolia, Kazakstan and to our delight, arrived intact. A computer centre was set up and the first ever email hub was established in the country. Even the UN and several embassies' personnel were making use of this service. Today it still offers free Internet access to the Tajik public. The team has grown to a point where some members now dedicate themselves to the other, equally important, ministry of birthing churches.

Creativity also means you have to adapt and become relevant. In one South Asian country OM has work in, the leaders came up with a novel and culturally acceptable idea of starting a beauty and hair salon for women. In a country where the male dominates, such an enterprise would not only offer the womenfolk privacy in their meeting together, follow-up and discipling work, it also guarantees them a hassle- and harassment-free informal ministry. No man would ever think of intruding and gate-crashing into a place which is the domain of women.

God is the Creator, therefore he is inherently creative. We are created beings – his creatures, given the ability to be creative. We are also his new creation, capable of even greater creativity. Don't say you are not creative. God has made us so, and it remains for us to use our creativity.

## Flexibility

The eighth quality, again not in order of preference, is that of flexibility. The dictionary says flexibility is that capability of bending without breaking. Not only is it not breakable, it has the ability to spring back with greater strength.

Flexibility is the appropriate response to continuous change. I often lament the fact that Singaporeans are not very good at being flexible. I am using Singaporeans as an example because I am familiar with our national and Christian traits. From my experience working with many cultures, this is probably true for other nationalities and cultures. Singaporeans have many good sides, but flexibility may not be one of them. We are over-conditioned, bureaucratic, too programme-, task- and result-oriented. Success is often measured by efficiency, punctuality and productivity. This is not bad in itself, but backfires when we impose our success formulas onto others without due consideration, understanding and sensitivity to their context. In missions, this is precisely the tendency of Singapore churches and missionaries.

Sagay, an Indian brother who coordinated the visit of a Singaporean-American medical team to India, was candid in illustrating this trait. While the American members were showing traits of their own, the Singaporeans were asking questions like – What is the programme tomorrow? What time is breakfast? If it is 7.30 a.m. in the morning, what time should we get up? The programme for the day was a talk to villagers about AIDS. More questions – How many villagers are expected? Will there be audio-visual equipment available? (in a simple Indian village?) What is the audience composition – how many male, female, adult and children? Sagay, apparently in exasperation, was gracious in his response: 'I don't have the answers to all your questions. If they come, they come. It doesn't matter what composition.'

I have found Paul's motto worth copying. In 1 Corinthians 9:22,23, he declares, 'I have become all things to all men so that by all possible means I might save some. I do all this for the sake of the gospel . . .' This is an interesting declaration when we consider the direct, pointed teachings Paul gave in his other epistles. Despite his firmness and bluntness, Paul had a flexible side to him.

In twenty-first century missions, flexibility is a requirement.

Kay (not her real name), is a Singaporean lady living and serving in one western Asian country for the past 12 years. For all these years, she has entered the country on a tourist visa. A tourist visa gives her three months' stay each time. When the three months expire, she is given an automatic extension of another three. At the end of (the maximum) six months, she leaves the country for a short trip to a neighbouring country. Upon her return, the cycle begins all over again. Yes, there is uncertainty in this approach but it has worked – all of 12 years. This involves a tremendous degree of flexibility. One is never sure how long such favour will be extended. Perhaps the immigration will catch up with her. Others I know working in the same country have student or work visas – just as valid a way to remain in the country.

## Resourcefulness

A resourceful person is one who has the skill in devising expedients. I have known people with this trait, and they are usually practical and smart. Besides being a practical trait, resourcefulness denotes one's inner strength and ingenuity. Ingenuity is one word I associate with resourcefulness. I like this word and the idea behind it. In the dictionary, ingenuity means inventiveness and cleverness. Sometimes, we come across an idea or product that is outstanding (normally in its originality and simplicity) and we know at once that the inventor is ingenious for designing it.

Third millennium missions can do with more resourceful people. The ministry of the MVs Doulos and Logos II are in need of people with practical resourcefulness. Once, while I was working as a deckhand on the Logos, Rory, the 3rd officer, assigned me a painting job. My job was to paint the confined spaces and recesses behind a series of pipes. Being one who liked to do a good job, I was frustrated by the difficulty in reaching behind the pipes. What I couldn't see I couldn't paint. It was simply impossible to squeeze into the tight space to see what I had missed. Rory, seeing my predicament, pulled out a mirror, placed it behind the pipe and showed me how easily it could be done with a bent brush. It had never occurred to me to use a mirror. An officer visiting from another ship remarked to Rory how impressed he was by the way I had used the mirror in one hand and a brush in the other! This was working smart, not working hard. Rory was working smart, while I was working hard.

In another incident, I was getting exasperated trying to unscrew a nut that was bolted dead on a metal socket. Try as I might, I just could not loosen the nut with a decent spanner. Dave Thomas, the chief engineer, happened to pass by, saw my problem and came to my rescue. He simply placed a pipe over the handle of the spanner to give it extra leverage. Instantly I heard a crack, and the nut was off. Engineers are smart too. That is why after thirty years, Dave is still the chief engineer on the MV Doulos and I am not!

Many works of God need people who are resourceful and practical. Are you such a person?

## Pioneering spirit

The last quality, but not the least, is that of a pioneering spirit. A pioneer is one who enters uncharted territory. In its old fashioned meaning, this refers to the explorer. In today's meaning, we can add the idea of an initiator; a person who initiates for others to follow. This is an extraordinary trait that only a few are endowed with.

Some ask the question, what unexplored places are there left in the world that need pioneers? Isn't the entire world known already? What or where remains unexplored? In missions, the same may also be asked. I have often been surprised that the average Christian has very little idea how unreached with the gospel a good part of the world is.

At the point of writing, I can easily name several countries where there is no indigenous church. This is due to adverse religious and political conditions. Pioneers who dare to take on some of these places are badly needed. OM has been invited to partner with the church in Mali (the country where Timbuktu is located) to start some pioneer work there. Workers needed must possess a pioneering streak because much of the country is desert. Little comfort is promised, and public conveniences will probably be non-existent.

Ping is a young man whom I prayed with several months ago before he left to serve in a country in Central Asia. We keep in contact and I maintain my prayer commitment to him. Soon after he was settled, he wrote: 'My current apartment looks like a bomb shelter. I have sporadic electricity, gas only in the evenings and the river off the tap. My tummy is coping well. Breakfast is rock-hard bread. Lunch is provided for US$1. Dinner is a science experiment every evening.' Despite the inconveniences, Ping requested prayer for spiritual maturity, daily understanding and insight to God's word, humility before him, love, patience and understanding within the team. But what encouraged me most was when he added: 'that I am willing to be broken for him to feed others.' This, then, is the pioneering spirit.

Paul again, is a fine example of a pioneer. He writes in Romans 15:20,21: 'It has always been my ambition to preach the gospel where Christ was not known, so that I would not be building on someone else's foundation. Rather as it is written: "Those who were not told about him will see, and those who have not heard will understand."'

That's it. All ten qualities describing the twenty-first century missionary.

How do you measure up? Have I described you? You don't have to possess all ten qualities – that would make you a Superman (or Superwoman) and superheroes are only cartoon characters that exist in comics. If you think you possess some (or a good chunk) of the qualities listed above, then I would say you have the potential, and may even make it as a missionary. If so, why not give it some thought and ask the Lord to show you how he can use you. But if you think the entire list describes you perfectly, then I would say you don't have a low-self image problem – you may want to add humility to the list!

These qualities are not elitist. I believe these are qualities that all Christians should have. As a matter of fact, all of us are gifted with some, if not all, of the above traits and qualities. It is now left to us to let God use us to fulfil his purpose.

# Chapter Eight

# Call waiting

I am going to share something daring in this chapter.

The subject in this chapter is about 'calling'.

I spoke on this subject on several occasions to mixed groups of missionaries and those aspiring to be missionaries. Their response has spurred me on to put this in writing. I am anticipating a reaction of the positive kind, but I am also ready if it sparks off a minor controversy as I bring a challenge to conventional wisdom on this subject.

Often the questions are asked – How does one receive a call from God in missions, or full-time Christian work? Is there a way to know for sure? I would like to be a missionary but God has not called, have I missed something?

If there are people who feel called to Christian service, there are also people who express in no uncertain terms that they don't feel called. However the same people who don't feel called to be a missionary cannot say for sure that God has called them to be something else – like a building contractor, an engineer, a teacher or a nurse.

Here's how I would define 'calling' – *it is a common assumption and belief that God speaks to people in an audible, unmistakable way, concerning one's life direction or vocation, normally in the context of full-time Christian work or to a life as a missionary.*

In grappling with this issue, I came up with no less than nine arguments against emphasising calling. Readers who have felt a definite call in their lives are exempted. I want you to know that I esteem and honour you for having received the call. My desire is to help many who are struggling with the call to understand perhaps there are other ways to interpret God's call.

Let me begin with the nine arguments.

The first argument is from *biblical injunction, or the lack of it*. There is an assumption that the Bible is filled with examples of people who are called. You have heard preachers preaching it and missionaries insisting on it (confession – I have done it myself!). It may be true that there are passages in the Bible recording individuals called to certain task – examples include Isaiah's call, Jonah's, Paul's Macedonian call. From them, we can learn some principles, but we stand in danger of being out of context if we apply such specific incidents to all situations, including our own. There is a tendency to read more into Scripture than it is intended.

Using computer Bible software, I was able to check on the word 'call' and its related applications – 'calling' and 'called'. What I found was interesting; there were few applications relating to what we understand calling to be.

So how did calling come about? My guess is that this was handed down from people in full-time ministry, and missionaries, through writings and the spoken word. Somewhere along the way, the jargon was used, accepted, adopted and perpetuated. Like some things in church history, when repeated often enough, alas, it becomes doctrine!

Let me quote from Christopher Chia, a pastor in Singapore, writing in the *Presbyterian News*: '*The main thrust of Pauline usage of "call" refers to God's objective divine call in Christ to salvation. Paul understands "calling" as the process by which God calls those whom he has elected and appointed out of bondage to this world so that he may save and sanctify them.*'

'Calling' in the Bible often refers to our higher calling in Christ; our position in Christ rather than our vocation. In Paul's time and context, the Christians were a minority suffering persecution, pressure, threats to their life and perhaps even suffering from a minority complex. Paul's exhortation was meant to uplift Christians living at that time. It was seldom referred to as a missionary call!

When Jesus issued the call to the disciples, it was a call to discipleship. Discipleship encompasses missions. Missions is not a separate subject but part of discipleship. Unfortunately, it is isolated in most churches where it becomes an optional extra or a stand alone component of church life.

The second argument is that *the interpretation is fuzzy*. The interpretations are many, and often unclear. When Christians say they are called they probably mean they have heard God's voice – that God speaks to them. Ask them how and they will say through Bible reading, through prayer, an unmistakable and audible voice, or through a chain of events that eventually leads to a decision to go full time in response to this call, or all the above.

Many believe that they must receive a clear call. Some missions insist on such a thing, including your spouse's if you are married. I suspect theological seminaries are not far behind in this requirement. Pastors, Christian leaders, missiologists and missionaries perpetuate this idea. Unless you have a definite call, they say, you will never be accepted into the organisation or seminary.

As a result, many are still waiting for the call. Perhaps you are too.

The third argument is a pragmatic one – *why apply the call only to the missionary and Christian enterprises, and not to other vocations?* Why be selective? Why single out the former and not the latter? Is it because the former is more noble and spiritual? What's wrong with being a full-time homemaker?

So we wait! We wait for a call to what, to where, how and when, few are sure.

In waiting, I believe many miss God's plan A. Here, I borrow a phrase from George Verwer, the founder of OM, who said that even if we missed God's plan A, B or C, he still has the entire alphabet!

The fourth argument is that in insisting on calling, *we leave all to God*. Isn't it right to leave all to God? When we say we leave all to God, there is no room left for counsel. If God has called you, then who are we to argue with you, or with God? If God has spoken, who are we to question? I want to tread carefully here. I believe that in the aspect of calling, it is not enough to 'hear' from God. This is because we are still very human, and in our humanity, we cannot say we can never be mistaken. Often we do misread God's word and mistake God's voice.

If your approach is 'I leave it all to God', you can get into a thorny situation. For instance, take the idea of marriage – what if some serious problems arise, and this happens even in the best of marriages, what do you say? 'Well,' you may say, 'God is solely responsible for my marriage. I left it all to him. Now that there are prob-lems, who else should I blame if not God?' It does not come as a surprise when couples spiritualise their failure this way. Blame it on God. This is not limited only to marriage. It can, and does, take place in missions.

When we leave all to God, and when things go wrong, we may be in danger of resenting God and everyone else.

I believe there must be personal commitment and responsibility, and not just leaving everything to God.

Fifthly, if we insist on calling, there lurks the danger of *shutting out the counsel of others that God may use in our lives*. The body of Christ is the place in which we will find the counsel of godly men and women, experienced and mature friends who can confirm, question or challenge our call. There is such a thing as accountability and I fear in our wilfulness we may ignore this safety net of godly counsel and participation.

My sixth argument is this – *a call is often the cause of missionary/ministry problem*. This is especially so when a person persists in outdated and outmoded ways. Such a person is either overstaying or over-extending his involvement. A person's stubbornness, character flaw, unwillingness to learn and to submit, are signs that this person is in the wrong ministry. But the fact that this person is called does not give him another option without the loss of face and embarrassment.

On the other hand, a person who genuinely feels that he does not fit may feel obligated to stay because he has received God's call. This person will feel a sense of guilt. He may also feel perhaps he has mistaken his wilfulness for God's call.

The seventh argument is that it is *easy to get stuck with a call*. Let's say you are called to a particular country. You finally get there and you are doing well in all aspects. But suddenly, things happen beyond your control – riots, impending war, visa problem, health, outbreak of violence or disease, or as it sometimes happens, your church recalls you because it needs your services. Incidentally, these are not hypothetical situations. You are faced with no alternative but to leave. Under such circumstances, missionaries leave their field of service prematurely. If this happens to you, how then would you explain your call? Did God, or did you, make a mistake?

If missionaries insist that God has called them to such and such a country, what happens when the country is closed to them? They are suddenly expelled. Again, is it a mistake?

My eighth point – if the Bible is not specific, *then our interpretation becomes subjective*. This means we can read into Scripture what we want and interpret passages to suit us. In determining a call, often personality plays a significant part. The more strong-minded or strong-headed a person is, the harder it is to change the mind once it is made up. Granted that a certain degree of doggedness is needed in pursuing missions, but the same persistence can elbow out the counsel of others or other things God is trying to say. If one has a strong personality, care must be taken so that one is also listening to others. Otherwise, one will fall into the trap of 'I have received the call, don't confuse me with the facts!'

When one refuses to be objective, when one insists on one's way, it can easily breed pride.

And finally, when we isolate the call to missions, *we ignore obedience to Jesus' command to go into all the world and make disciples*. Jesus' command is for us to obey. The command is already given in three of the four Gospels and again in Acts 1:8. What is needed for all of us is to heed and obey.

Now that I have said what I want to say in argument against calling, let me respond to the three points commonly used to support calling.

One, without a call, one will not last in missions or full-time ministry. When the pressures come and when you don't have a definite call to fall back on, the argument goes, you will opt out. To counter this point, I would say this – most Christians are in vocations (outside of full-time) without a call anyway, but they have lasted! Just talk to your Christian friends to find out if this is the case. In my case, I don't remember receiving a clear and definite call to missions, but I have lasted almost thirty years.

Two, getting a call is biblical. I have mentioned this in my first argument against calling. Let me repeat, it is often the principles and not the specifics we can apply. We need to understand how to apply biblical examples correctly. If we don't, we will be out of context, and this can cause theological problems. Try applying Paul's example to yourself directly; you will need to be blinded for three days!

Three, so many people can't be wrong. True. Let me reiterate, I am not against calling. I admire those who are clearly called. What I am trying to do is to bring some balance to this notion in the hope that the average Christian will also experience the same resolve and commitment even if they don't get called. Those of us who have not received a call need not feel intimidated by those who have.

What is the way ahead? Can a person be called? Of course. In that case, do we have to wait for the call to come? No, you don't have to.

Here's what I propose – firstly, recognise that it is *a problem of semantics*. Change the language. Don't say 'I am waiting for a call', 'God has not called (yet)', 'One must be called' or similar expressions. Use other expressions that communicate more accurately – like 'I am committed to missions', 'I obey the Lord's command unreservedly', 'I feel led to be a missionary in such and such a country', 'I may not have received a call but I am sold out to God's purpose'.

Secondly, recognise that *God works in people differently.* We are all different. God may give a loud call to some, or he may speak in a still small voice (more likely) to others. If you are the reading type, God will probably speak to you through the printed page. The printed page, especially the word of God, comes across clearer to us than through our listening faculty. Also, to those short of wisdom, God often speaks through the wisdom of others, young and old.

Thirdly, *people don't need a call as much as they need guidance.* Even when one claims to have received the 'call', one still needs guidance to confirm that call. Calling is a process. In such a process, guidance is needed. Missions is far more than just a calling. Personal issues are involved. If you are married, children's issues like their education, development and career are major concerns. Economics also come in to play. Often I find people unrealistic about economics in missions. Yes, faith is important, but not at the expense of common sense.

Fourthly, *'commitment'* is a better concept than 'calling'. There is something solid, reliable, dependable and enduring in the meaning of commitment. I have admitted that I did not have a clear call to missions. But my commitment, since the age of eighteen, had grown, and is still growing. If I were called at eighteen, I could have lasted, I guess, but still there were factors that had come into play for the commitment to grow. Here's one of my few original statements – *guidance means you can count on God (and his people); commitment means God can count on you.* Whether we are called or not, we must be committed.

Lastly, and probably most importantly, *the role of the church.* When we act alone, we act against the

structure/body God has set up in which we must function. If we are mature, wise and esteeming enough, we
will want to work through the church, especially our
home church. When the entire church is involved –
including the church leaders – the chances of success,
better pastoral care and counsel, prayer, moral and
financial support are that much higher. It is true that in
missions history, the church might have been slow, and
if not for stubborn and strong-willed, called pioneers,
the church and missions would not be where they are
today. We have such pioneers to thank. But in this day
and age, I believe the church has an extremely important
role to play and we do well to involve, and consult with,
them. This is proper team work, not solo enterprise with
its negative implications.

Let me bring this chapter to a close. Essentially, I don't
see missions (outside of full-time ministry in the
church), as an option. The Lord has given a command
clear as a bell, to his disciples. He didn't mention any
exceptions. To all his disciples, he said 'go'. Some go to
their neighbours, while others go further afield. This is
not the issue. The issue is that we obey his command.

God's purpose in missions involves the whole church.
This involves team work. Romans 10:14,15 emphasises
the role of the 'sender', whereas traditionally, missionaries emphasise the 'goer'. But how can they go unless
they are sent by the body of Christ, the church?

God has commanded. Don't wait for his call – this has
been given a long time ago. What we need to know is
our specific roles as senders.

## Chapter Nine

# Missions – off the charts!

I have bad news.

The bad news concerns missions.

Jesus Christ gave the church the Great Commission 2,000 years ago, but missions has still not made it to the 'pop charts' of the average church and the average Christian. By average church, I mean the normal, Bible-believing church of Jesus Christ and by the average Christian, I mean the normal, Bible-believing, re-born Christian. There are exceptions, but I am talking about the average.

Why has missions not hit it big in the church? Why, after two millennium, has a third or more of the world still not been reached with the gospel and untold numbers perish by the day without ever knowing Jesus as their Saviour?

In this chapter, I want to suggest ten reasons for the demise of missions.

**Reason No. 1**
**Missions is not popular because celebration is**

This is a no-brainer. Anyone can tell you that Celebration is on the 'pop charts' of the church. It will always remain on the 'Top 10 Hit List' of the church. And missions? It is hardly worth a mention. If it is, it is usually relegated to the once-a-year missions emphasis week or something similar.

Missions conferences don't attract people. OK, I have heard of Urbana and how it attracts as many as 20,000 to each tri-annual gathering; I have heard of Missions Korea, and lately Singapore's Go4th National Missions Conference. But what is that compared to a Christian pop concert held anywhere, anytime, in any part of the world where there is a sizeable church! People pay to attend events where there is celebration. Thousands travel from far and wide to get to Christian pop or rock festivals, revival events, healing services, or to get a chance to listen to some famous speakers, or to listen to their favourite band. Please understand that I am not against such events – I go to some of them myself. There is a place for it. But why so many go for these and few, often the die-hards, are motivated enough to attend a missions conference? Organisers often resort to last minute begging and pleading with the Christian public to come to missions events. Incentives, like full or partial sponsorship, will not make a big difference in attendance. The average missions conference is unattractive and poorly attended. Maybe as missionaries, we are to be blamed. We simply do not stand a chance with the competition.

Worship events, celebration, concerts, or whatever name they are creatively given, draw crowds because they are positive and attractive events. The worship leader is usually a talented artiste with several CDs to his credit, the music is outstanding and so are the musicians. Back up singers are pretty and their voices blend well. The sound system is faultless and the ambience is just right. Songs sung are contemporary, hip, soothing, personal, applicable and sing-able. Overall, the perform-ance is impeccable. The volume may be a bit loud for some but hey, who is complaining, everyone is having a great time and the feeling all round is good. More importantly, the Lord is worshipped.

The added bonus is that you feel anonymous. You feel safe being anonymous. Big concerts and events do that to you. There is no pressure to get to know people, to catch up with regular church folks, to have to answer awkward and uncomfortable questions, especially when your life has not been so good lately. You are just one of many nobodies and there is no need to pretend or to hide.

As if this is not enough, there is the speaker – they are the icing on the cake and they are something else. Skilful orator, motivator and inspirer. With a gift of healing, it can only be a winner. Having worshipped and heard God's word, all this contributes to a general state of all-round wellness. Spiritually you are edified and physi-cally – well, your sickness may even get healed. At the end you leave the meeting feeling well in your spirit and body. You have just enjoyed a good bless-up! No wonder thousands go for it.

Missions conferences, on the other hand, are almost the opposite. Under-budgeted (since many are not will-ing to pay to come), there are not many state-of-the-art effects. Missionaries, alas, are not some of the most fash-ionable (and attractive? Attractiveness, we console our-selves, is what is inside) people to draw the crowds. It is hard to find a worship band and singers with a reper-toire of popular contemporary missions songs to add value to the event. Most of the time, old hymns written two or three hundred years ago are sung. While some of these songs are great and rich in meaning, most are still foreign, unfamiliar or simply old fashioned. It is not easy to get people roused in enthusiasm.

Missionaries are often not the best communicators or storytellers. Many are modest and humble about their work and achievements. Audio visuals they use may not be the most high-tech. Missions displays are unimaginative and low-budget, resulting in few even bothering to view such displays. This can be depressing.

Missions conferences and events are uncomfortable and awkward. They are always talking about spiritual needs and suffering and the audience end up feeling guilty for not going or giving enough.

Missions conferences and events are especially risky because you may even get 'called' into missions. Calling is the last thing you want. We all know that this will only cause an upheaval in our lives, plans and careers. Even if we don't get called, missions challenges tend to rattle and unsettle most of us.

Something else about missions conferences and events which is most insensitive and inconsiderate – they tell you it is too early to celebrate! How can you celebrate when so much of the world is yet unreached with the gospel?

**Reason No. 2**
**Missions fatigue**

People do get tired of missions.

I believe this has to do with our result-orientation. We want quick and immediate results in missions. We invest money, and we expect returns – isn't this good business sense? The trouble is, missions is not a business. Cause and effect does not work in all situations here. Some countries and ministries have not yielded any significant results in terms of increase in the Christian population despite years of time, energy, prayer and effort. We measure effectiveness and productivity by the results, but some mission fields are hard and unproductive grounds. I know many works of God will not yield quick results. I am not saying we do not expect results – of course we do. But realism is needed here – there are many godly, faithful groups, labouring in countries where they have yet to see any major breakthroughs. Be careful of missions preachers who claim simplistic answers or offer formulas for just the breakthrough needed. This can smack of arrogance.

When the results are not obvious after all the investment of people, time and money, people get tired. And churches get tired too.

Churches get tired especially when there is seemingly no direct benefit from the 'investment'. Why give people and money to far away and remote places like Ethiopia or Tibet when it is obvious we will not get any returns? Also, bad experiences in missions can leave a bad taste in the mouth and the relationship between churches and mission agencies has often soured and suffered as a result. No wonder churches give up on missions.

**Reason No. 3**
**Missions intimidation**

I blame this on missions speakers, missionaries and books on missions and about missionaries. Intentionally or unintentionally, the message that missions is elitist is conveyed to the average Christian listener and reader. I am all too familiar with missions speakers (I include myself) who paint such a high calling and sacred approach to missions. The average Christian comes to the conclusion that one must be so spiritual, so sinless, so holy, so sensitive, so prayerful, so full of faith, vision and conviction before one even considers applying to join a two week mission trip!

Try asking the average Christian to be involved in missions, and you will get responses like: 'I don't think I am ready', 'I am not trained', 'I am not sure', 'I don't sense the call', 'I cannot make the sacrifice yet', 'I am still young', 'I am too old already' and so on. It is not uncommon to meet potential missionaries who are still preparing and waiting for the perfect time to become one after five or seven years!

People are scared stiff of missions because we have the habit of scaring them away.

### Reason No. 4
### Concerns centring around self

People are concerned about the immediate and what is closest to them. Family, children, career, work, church all take up much of our time and energy. Such concerns are legitimate and necessary. But these can be overwhelming, and often sap our energy and resources to a point that leaves little else for missions. Missions, as a result, is elbowed right to an inconspicuous corner of many church programmes.

Some churches do not even have a missions department while in others, the committee has difficulty sustaining its own commitment and interest. At any rate, the church is overtaken by, and over-committed to, urgent local concerns and needs. Missions can wait.

A young lady, serving as a missionary in another country, received no financial support from her home church. It was not because the church could not afford it; it was reasonably wealthy. Upon completion of her commitment, she returned home but continued serving in the mission's home office. She also became one of the pioneer members of her home church missions committee. At one committee meeting, as the financial policy was being fine tuned, her pastor asked, out of curiosity, how much did the church support her while overseas. 'Nothing,' she replied. She survived only on the goodwill of some friends and family members, and in the process learned immensely about God's faithfulness. When the pastor heard this, he literally broke down and wept. He felt so ashamed that they had neglected their own member. To make amends, the church backdated her support for half if not the entire time.

The story didn't end there; when the missions committee proposed the first missions emphasis month in the church calendar, there was resistance. Why emphasise missions when there was a great need in the Christian education and worship departments? And on it went. Again to her credit and courage, this young lady responded with something like: 'In all the twenty or more years of our church's existence, there has never been a lack of emphasis on the different departments; don't you think it is about time to give missions a chance?' Thankfully, this church has since grown in its responsibility and maturity in missions.

**Reason No. 5
Over-familiarity with missions**

Missions interest is hard to sustain. Coupled with the fact that most missionaries leave and serve in other countries, 'out of sight is out of mind'. If you find a church actively concerned and interested in its missionaries, it is a real encouragement.

In this day and age of instant news, missions news by contrast is slow and months late. It used to be the missions organisations that monopolised, hoarded or supplied exclusive missions news, but not so today. The average person hears it quicker than us. It doesn't matter if the news informs as much as it misinforms!

Why should mission agencies be surprised that others have already received the information and have overtaken us in coming up with the answers to the needs? Why should we be taken aback when what we think is new is actually old hat? I believe this is a very healthy challenge for missionaries to be up-to-date in our news, to be fresh and relevant in our ministries. I believe this is one way to fight over-familiarity. God is at work in all the news – even if it doesn't sound like God is involved! He surely must, and so we need to discern and find out what he is doing in the hot spots of the world. One must never become over-familiar with the way God works.

'Knowledge is a good thing; but a little knowledge is dangerous,' someone has said. A little knowledge is a dangerous thing. A little is not much, it is not complete and it may even be out of context. And if we are not careful, it may lead to false or misinformation. And that is a dangerous thing. Missions is not spared from people who have little knowledge but think they are experts. Some church missions policies reflect such a lack of knowledge. Ministries have suffered and even been jeopardised due to insufficient knowledge.

## Reason No. 6
## Lack of information and awareness

I have become keenly aware of this as I meet and talk with many pastors. Pastors, with their heavy load of pastoral duties and care for the flock, have little time and energy left for missions. Coupled with a lack of information, missions inevitably gets neglected. Pastors are often the key to church missions involvement, but when pastors fail to lead in this area, the church automatically suffers from missions ignorance. Missions awareness consequently suffers a decline and an eventual demise.

I just returned from a trip to the Caribbean to visit the MV Logos II. It was my first time in the Caribbean and so you could imagine how much I was looking forward to it. I had promised Lawrence Tong, the ship director, that I would pay a visit to bring encouragement to the crew and staff on board. The ship was visiting St Kitts and Nevis. I was delighted to be given an hour to speak to the pastors and Christian leaders at both places.

Nevis has an island population of 11,000. The churches number 52. The average attendance per church is 100. This works out to be 5,200 church-goers, or 47 per cent of the population! In St Kitts, the population is 31,000 with 140 churches. The rough average is 100 per church. At 14,000 church-goers, the percentage is about 45 per cent. These percentages are high in comparison to most countries in the world.

As I continued, I counted only a handful out of the total of 60 pastors and Christian leaders who knew what the '10/40 window' referred to. Asked if any church represented had missionaries overseas, all said no. Some pastors had come from other islands to serve in Nevis and St Kitts. When I continued in my message, I had a distinct sense that what I thought were common news and views, were in fact new to them. They had never heard about the needs of the world and so had little awareness.

After my message, Mukadum, a young lady from Uzbekistan, came on with an Uzbek dance. She then shared how she got saved in Uzbekistan and how the

Lord led her to be involved with missions. I thought
Mukadum was a powerful illustration that if the Uzbek
church, which is small and struggling, could send one,
then St Kitts and Nevis really have no excuse.

Pastors, if you are reading this, I exhort you to take
the lead. You may not be able to do everything, but the
least you can do is to empower your members.
Encourage them in creative ways in motivating the
church. Christians often lament the fact that their pastors and church leaders provide little support to missions, and this is discouraging.

**Reason No. 7**
**Lack of interest**

Sadly, there is a big percentage of Christians who basically have no interest in missions. I don't want to be
hard on them. Sometimes, I wonder if the apathy is conditioned by affluence.

This piece of humour has been in circulation – an
interviewer who is appalled by the ignorance and apathy of Christians comes up to one to ask why this is so.
The Christian promptly replies, 'I don't know and I
don't care!'

The fault is not a lack of information on missions, nor
a lack of accessibility to agencies.

I speak on missions all the time in churches around
Asia. I can be as passionate as I want to be in my preaching. The expression on the faces of listeners may register
understanding. But on average, I get only one or two
people coming up to ask me about missions after the
meetings. It may be in a church of 100 or 500. The
response is quite pathetic and discouraging. Once, I was
speaking in a large church. After the service, only one

person came up to me to say hello. Maybe they were all shy. But all 400 of them? The members were all busy catching up with one another over a cup of coffee. I have not given up on the church. I am still speaking in church after church, meeting after meeting, laying brick after brick, in the hope and prayer that the little I do will make a difference in missions.

**Reason No. 8**
**Fear of suffering and sacrifice**

People admire missionaries. As soon as they hear you are one, they imagine you are like Mother Teresa, Hudson Taylor or David Livingstone. They look up to missionaries for their willingness and courage to give up everything in order to serve the Lord in another country – somewhere remote, primitive, unreachable, or mosquito-infested.

In considering missions, Christians imagine too much! In their imagination, they come to the conclusion that they are not ready to sacrifice, suffer and die in the mission field. They only remember the few who died, but the majority who made it back safe and sound is conveniently forgotten.

Another disincentive to join missions is the poor job prospects after that. In the first place, missions is voluntary. Almost all agencies do not pay their missionaries. You need to raise your own funds and support for your missions career. The average Christian is unfamiliar with this ethos in missions. Prospective missionaries often ask how much the pay cheque is. Missions is hard to understand for the world at large. The chances of getting a job after being a missionary are slim; that missionaries are unemployable is a   misconception. Former missionaries are some of the best employees for any out-fit that wants to employ them. They have cross-cultural experience, and are usually proficient in several languages. They have integrity and know how to relate to internationals. And you will be surprised to know that missionaries often have quite advanced skills and technological know-how.

### Reason No. 9
### Prejudice

Prejudice has been around for as long as human beings have been around. Prejudice is inborn in human beings. It is a sin that breeds easily among Christians. The good news is that it is possible to unlearn prejudice.

Prejudice rears its ugly head among Christians in the form of racism, ethnocentricity and favouritism. Jesus abhorred that and so did Paul. If you think this does not happen in the church, then we are probably not on the same planet. What would happen if a person in leather jacket, tattoos, metal studs, bleached hair, holding a cigarette were to walk into our church? Some people would have a mild heart attack. Some would feel awkward and would not know how to relate. There will certainly be murmurs.

Prejudice in the church affects missions. Churches have preference. They would rather reach their own kind with the gospel. Reasons for this? Well, reaching out to that other group will only cause problems – can you not tell by their culture and behaviour? Also, can you not see there has been animosity and differences between us? Somehow, this kind of behaviour does not tally with the gospel of unconditional love.

**Reason No. 10**
**Financial constraint**

Missions is costly. Not just in terms of lives, but in terms
of money. Some people think that because missions is
done in a country where the cost of living is lower, it
ought to be cheap. There is a prevalent call proposing
the only way forward is to hire local workers. The
rationale is that national workers are a lot cheaper. Why
send foreigners who cost so much more than locals?
Joseph de Souza, my good friend and colleague who
heads up the work of OM India with 1,200 workers,
called this a scandal. It is insulting even to infer that
such workers can be hired for a few dollars.

Missions is not cheap. It never has been. For this reason, some economically poorer countries that are rich in
missionary potential, cannot afford to send missionaries.
Living and working overseas cost a lot more than
remaining at home. Just the start up, even in the 'cheap-
est' country, will cost.

For many years, it has been disheartening to see many
potential missionaries in the Philippines, Indonesia,
Myanmar and Papua New Guinea missing the opportunity to serve the Lord in other more spiritually needy
places because there is not enough money to send them.
Despite the fact that agencies have lowered their cost for
these, the minimum livable amount is still way beyond
their affordability. For instance, the OM ships only require
a minimum of US$200-250 per month for third world mis-
sionaries to live and work on board. This amount is very
low by normal standard, but the pastors of these potential
missionaries don't even get half of this amount as their
salary. It is way beyond the reach of some churches.

Then again, the Lord didn't say to go into all the
world only when you have the money. Interestingly,

despite the complaint about not having enough money to support missions, the same people have no difficulty in finding the money to go on holidays abroad.

The ten reasons above can be daunting. But take heart, they are not insurmountable. We will have to persevere and continue to speak out for missions if we are serious about fulfilling our part in the Great Commission.

# Chapter Ten

# Missions, top hit!

If missions is not happening in the average church, what can we do to reverse this? And if missions is not in the mind of the average Christian, how can we change that?

In this chapter, I want to convince you and the church about the need for missions. If you and your church are already well on your way, perhaps you don't need to read this chapter. But there is really no harm in revisiting the why we are supposed to be involved in missions.

Let's look at seven reasons why we need to put missions back on the Hit List.

## Hit No. 1
## Because of God's glory

At the first national missions conference held in Singapore recently, Bob Sjogren enlightened the 3,000 missions enthusiasts with his vivid session on a re-look at Scripture. He convinced the audience that the Bible is not about us, but is all about God. Beginning from the account of creation in Genesis chapter 1, Sjogren highlighted God's own response to his creation. At the end of each of the six days of creation, God saw that it was good. He was pleased with what he himself had created. He took pleasure in what he had done. The glory was his alone. Then Sjogren opened up the rest of Scripture to point out the references that confirmed his proposition that the Bible is all about God's glory. Even the most central event of the Bible – Jesus' death on the cross, was an event where God was glorified (Jn. 17:1-3). Revelation, the last book of the Bible, which is a book about the end times and the consummation of creation and humankind, points us to the main focus, God. Not humankind, or creation.

God's purpose is grand, majestic, brilliant, infinitely wise and of such a magnitude that finite beings like us can never properly or fully comprehend it. The Bible says that even with the help of the Holy Spirit, it will take eternity to fathom God's love alone! (Eph. 3:18,19; Rom. 8:38,39).

Suffice it to say that as Christians, we must be concerned, first and foremost, about bringing glory to God. Firstly, in our lives – how we live and behave, and in our engagement in fulfilling his purpose for the world.

The chief end of humankind is to glorify God. This is the single most important thing to do but alas, it is all too easily lost in the hustle and bustle of life. And in the same hustle and bustle, his grand purpose for the world is lost to us.

## Hit No. 2
### God's purpose is to give eternal life to all people

The Lord Jesus opened his prayer to the Father with this: 'For you granted him authority over all people that he might give eternal life to all those you have given him.

Now this is eternal life: that they may know you, the only true God, and Jesus Christ, whom you have sent.' (Jn. 17:2,3, NIV)

In this prayer we are privileged to hear in Jesus' own words his motivation and reason for coming down from heaven. Jesus was sent by his Father. It was the Father's initiative and Jesus' willingness and obedience (Phil. 2:6-8).

What a grand plan of love and sacrifice by both the Father and the Son.

Missions, in its simplest form, is to introduce people to Jesus so that they may have eternal life, enjoy fellowship with and worship the Triune God. It does not matter what approaches or methods people may use, the hope and prayer and heartfelt desire is for this to take place. Whether it is through aid, development, crisis and emergency relief, or day-to-day plodding on in Bible translation or teaching people to read, our deepest desire must be in line with the Triune God.

## Hit No. 3
## Jesus lived and died to save the world

Jesus is God. He did not consider equality with God something to be grasped, but made himself nothing, like a servant. In his incarnation, he took upon himself the limitations of a man. He did not stop there, but humbled himself and became obedient to death – even to the most excruciating form of death known at that time. (See Phil. 2:6,8, NIV)

Colossians 1:20 says 'and through him (Christ) to reconcile to himself (God) all things, whether things on earth or things in heaven, by making peace through his blood, shed on the cross.'

This is what I called love beyond comprehension. Even as I write this, my heart wells up in worship and I feel I am not doing justice to such an important and significant truth with a few short sentences. But I trust you will grasp my point about getting involved in the life-saving profession.

I could stop here. The three 'hits' above are enough to convince me about my involvement. I hope you are convinced too. But in case these three points are too lofty, the rest will bring it down to a more understandable and practical level.

## Hit No. 4
## Because God says so in the Bible

In the above three 'hits', we understand the specific desire and work of the Father and the Son. They have played their part in the divine purpose and they have played it fully and completely. They held nothing back. In addition to that, the Father and the Son have left very specific instructions to the disciples, and to Christians like you and me. It is for us to obey. Let's look at several key passages with these instructions. I have deliberately chosen the ones spoken by Jesus after his resurrection and before his ascension. The last instructions before he left the earth are probably some of the most important.

*Matthew 28:18-20* – 'All authority in heaven and on earth has been given to me. Therefore go and make disciples of all nations, baptising them in the name of the Father and of the Son and of the Holy Spirit, and teaching them to obey everything I have commanded you. And surely I am with you always, to the very end of the age.' (NIV)

Commonly known as the Great Commission given by Jesus, this passage is pretty comprehensive. Christians are commissioned with his authority. Our mandate is to make disciples, baptising and teaching them – essentially this describes the enterprise of starting churches. The scope is 'all nations', or peoples (not just countries). And we have Jesus' promise of his presence. This is a powerful and power-packed passage indeed. With such resources, there is very little else that we need!

*Mark 16:15,16* – 'Go into all the world and preach the good news to all creation. Whoever believes and is baptised will be saved, but whoever does not believe will be condemned.' (NIV)

The word 'go', I believe, has been the definitive command that has mobilised thousands of missionaries in church and missions history.

*Acts 1:8* – 'But you will receive power when the Holy Spirit comes on you; and you will be my witnesses in Jerusalem, and in all Judea and Samaria, and to the ends of the earth.'

This verse, spoken just before his ascension, is especially urgent. It traces the movement of the gospel outward from Jerusalem. After the first few years, the gospel spread to Samaria. Paul broke through to the Gentiles and in his generation, much of Asia Minor was reached with the gospel. Since then, almost two thousand years later, we are still trying to fulfil the last part of this verse 'to the ends of the earth'. We are not there yet. We still have some way to go.

*1 Timothy 2:5,6* – 'For there is one God and one mediator between God and men, the man Christ Jesus, who gave himself as a ransom for all men . . .'

Salvation is in no one else except Jesus. There is only one mediator. Christ is unique in what he did and why he did it. In this age of religious tolerance and religious correctness, it is easy to dilute the strength of this statement. Be careful that you don't fall prey to the popular idea that 'all religions are the same and they all lead to God.' To say that is to admit your ignorance about religions. Religions don't lead to God – some even lead to self. We have a unique message that will meet the deepest longing of the human heart.

*Romans 10:15* – 'How beautiful are the feet of those who bring good news!'

So we've got it all wrong! It's not 'how beautiful are the faces, or body, or even the hair!' The world places far too much importance on faces. God places beauty on, of all places, the feet! Why feet? I have always wondered about this. It seems God has a sense of humour. Feet are not beautiful. If you don't believe me, just take a closer look at your feet. Do you not agree?

Well, God disagreed. He said that beautiful are the feet of those who bring good news. The qualification here is 'who bring good news'. If you are engaged in bringing good news to others, then your feet are a beauty. Feet denote action. If we keep busy on our feet, and we are up and about with the good news, God said our feet are beautiful. Don't forget, Jesus stooped down to wash the disciples' feet.

Bible verses on missions are not out of fashion. Just because we think they are over-used or over-quoted, we should not surmise that God cannot speak to us any more. I believe he does.

**Hit No. 5**
**Because God is still working**

John wrote in his gospel chapter 21:25: 'Jesus did many other things as well. If every one of them were written down, I suppose that even the whole world would not have room for the books that would be written.'

The Gospels recorded only a short account of Jesus life and what he did. John said that there was a lot more unrecorded. For that matter, the Bible does not contain everything that God did. It would have been impossible anyway. God is still working!

And if God is still working then the wisest thing to do is to work in tandem with him!

How does God work? Through his Church. OK, maybe not all churches, but who are we to judge? God can work in all kinds of situations, even in seemingly dead churches. It is far too easy to put blame on the church. Remember, you are part of the church. If you blame the church, you are blaming yourself.

The church is the bride of Christ, and Christ is ever preparing the bride – purifying her, sanctifying her through the Holy Spirit. And Christ is ever expanding the Church. '. . . I will build my church, and the gates of Hades will not overcome it.' (Mt. 16:18, NIV)

Some churches in some countries may appear to be fighting a losing battle, but this is not the overall picture. Ultimately, the overall picture is going to be positive. Revelation 7:9,10 gives us a picture of a great multitude that no one could count, from every nation, tribe, people and language, standing before the throne and in front of the Lamb. It will happen. It is only a matter of time, and it will take a final surge of effort by the churches around the world to see this happen.

## Hit No. 6
## Because we will be held accountable

The Bible teaches clearly about accountability.

Look at Matthew 25, the parable of the talents. This parable teaches us about good and bad stewards. Good stewards are those who put their talents to good use. Bad stewards are those who do not put their talents to any use at all.

This parable teaches us that good stewards will receive their reward; bad stewards will receive judgement. This is a serious teaching that invokes a serious response. The parable, therefore, emphasises the principle, 'from the one who has been entrusted with much, much more will be asked' (Lk 12:48, NIV).

Whether we have little or much, we have to account for it someday. Rather than complaining about the little, we should be finding ways to use it for the glory of God. Neither envy those who have much nor those who have little. We are all held accountable for what we are given.

Then there is the teaching about gifting in Ephesians chapter 4. We are all part of the body of Christ. Not all are hands, not all are heads; all are different and function differently. We are all gifted in different ways and in different things. No one is gifted with all the gifts. Don't ask the Lord for all the gifts – that's being greedy! When we are gifted in some areas, it naturally implies that we are not gifted in other areas. Therefore we will be dependent on other's gifting to help us grow. The purpose is to build up and to grow up the body. The chapter teaches that in using our gift, we grow. Unfortunately some Christians never grow up because they have withheld the use of their gift.

Granted, not all are gifted with the missionary gift. Peter Wagner suggests that there is such a thing as the missionary gift. A person with this gift has the ability to relate cross-culturally, adapt and be effective in communicating the gospel. I tend to agree with Wagner. If you are not gifted as such, that's fine. You will then have to find out what part you can play. In the next chapter, I have some practical suggestions for the non-missionary types to help them fulfil their role as supporters.

**Hit No. 7**
**Because the challenge still remains**

Consider these facts:
- there are only three workers for every million Muslims (1.2 billion)
- there are only five workers for every million Buddhists (400 million)
- there are only five workers for every million Hindus (820 million)
- there are over one hundred and eighty-five Christian workers for every million people who claim to be Christians

These figures show the great imbalance. Much of the world is still waiting to hear the gospel for the first time. We need to correct this disparity in the mission force.

Paul was spot-on with this principle: 'It has always been my ambition to preach the gospel where Christ was not known, so that I would not be building on someone else's foundation. Rather, as it is written: "Those who were not told about him will see, and those who have not heard will understand."' Rom. 15:20,21

Paul's view was simple and logical – preach the gospel where Christ was not known. During Paul's time it was said that the whole province of Asia heard. (See Acts 19:10) Later, it was he and his small team who brought the gospel to Europe. We do well in emulating Paul's pioneering passion.

Let me conclude this chapter with an excerpt from a pledge that was said at the recent Go4th National Missions Conference held in tiny Singapore. It beautifully conveys what I am trying to put across.

The three thousand or so attendants pledged:

- Because I am uniquely and wonderfully made by God my father, for purposes prepared for me before I was born,
- Because I have received Jesus Christ as my sovereign Lord and Saviour,
- Because I am called to live for God's missions, rather than for my own ambitions,
- Because all humanity is eternally lost apart from Jesus,
- Because this gospel of the kingdom must be preached in all the world as a witness to all peoples,
- Because Jesus is worthy of worship by every nation, people, tribe and tongue.

I commit my entire life to obey the Lord of the Harvest whenever he calls, wherever he leads, and however he positions me.

I will give primary consideration to the places and peoples currently beyond the reach of the gospel – to spread the fame of his name for the unveiling of his glory!

More impressed by the greatness of my God than by the size of the challenge before me, I will impart vision and inspire my generation to care and to dare. Together, we will serve with compassion in our window in time.

Let's work together to bring missions back on the charts.

# Chapter Eleven

# For non-missionaries

You are honest about it.

You are pretty sure you are not the missionary type. You have come this far in the book and you have no problem with much of what I have said. But you still prefer to stay put. You feel your place is more or less where you are. That's fine.

I have written about the importance of being a sender. Let me begin by re-affirming that a sender (one who sends, or supporter) is not a class lower than the goer (the one sent, or missionary). The missionary-sender is not less than the missionary. The two form one team. One cannot do without the other. Both are crucial to the success of the missions enterprise. I cannot emphasise enough the importance of both roles.

But what is the sender's role? Neal Pirolo's book *Serving as Senders*[3] has become the essential handbook for the average non-missionary type in the church. Much of what I am proposing is not far off the target from Pirolo's.

---

[3] Neal Pirolo, *Serving as Senders* (Emmaus Road International)

## 1. Make a conscious decision

You must make a conscious decision to be a sender or supporter. Be a fan of missions. A fan is short for fanatic. Soccer has its fanatics, golf has its fanatics, so what's wrong with missions having some enthusiasts of its own? Sign up as a 'club' member. Make this decision asap. Say to yourself, 'I want in!' For too long, Christians have procrastinated. Wait for the appropriate time and day, they say. There is never a more opportune time then now! You are not making a decision to go to the moon. It is actually a simple decision you are making which has positive and significant repercussions in someone's life. It will enrich yours immeasurably.

## 2. Be faithful in prayer

Matthew 9:37,38: 'The harvest is plentiful but the workers are few. Ask the Lord of the harvest to send our workers into his harvest field.' (NIV) You have an important job cut out for you already. This prayer request the Lord himself instructed is still being answered. There are never enough workers! Your first job is to pray to the Lord of the harvest to send.

There will be no lack of missionaries and missions to pray for. The challenge is to keep abreast of the prayer requests and to follow through to see they are being answered. Sometimes, without finding out the outcome, people continue to pray for things that had either taken place or expired. This is prayer wasted. Pray hard, yes, but pray smart too.

## 3. Make it a habit to give

This is perhaps the most common and practical expression of your seriousness about missions. Give to your church by all means. But give also to missions. Acts 20:35 exhorts: 'It is more blessed to give than to receive.' (NIV) Christians turn it around and say 'it is more blessed to receive than to give!' In giving, you are doing what Matthew 6:20 is saying, you 'store up for yourselves treasures in heaven. . . .'(NIV)

Don't be intimidated by big givers. Normal givers suffer from low self-esteem when they feel their giving is small compared to others. What can God do with so little, they wonder. But never doubt that God can use whatever the amount when it is given from the heart. Don't forget to train children to give. Some of our kids have so much that they need to learn to give. Cultivate generosity.

Points 2 and 3, to pray and give, are the two most basic actions you can take. It is not a lot that the Bible is asking for, is it? But let me assure you that it will take you a lifetime to practise it! The same is true for most of the basic teaching in the Bible.

## 4. Stay motivated and committed to the task

Even the best efforts can fall foul to over-exposure and exhaustion. Pace your involvement. Don't bite off more than you can chew. Be realistic in your ability to handle small jobs and commitments. Just as missionaries can experience burnout, so can supporters back home. Never underestimate the intensity of the work of a sender/supporter.

Keep the flame of interest burning with stories, news and testimonies from the fields and the missionaries. When things are getting tough for the missionaries in the field – this can be due to many things, like crisis, war, emergency, threat – this is when your commitment counts. Don't back out of it when your help is most needed.

## 5. Compassionate action

Compassion transcends distance. One does not have to live among the poor and unfortunate to feel compassion for them. It is helpful being with them of course, but if you cannot be there, let your compassion motivate you to action. I have known people whose help is critical to those in compassionate ministry. When there is a special need, these people are quick in raising the funds and the materials needed, out of their compassion and this is truly commendable.

## 6. Material support is crucial to long-term work

When my family was living in Hong Kong, someone paid for my children's education. This took a load off our shoulders. That person knew how grateful we were for her generosity. Another person became our power of attorney in our absence. I remember when my son was waiting for a place in the school just before our return. Our power of attorney went for the ballot and was delighted that my son's name was among the first to be called, thus securing a place in the popular school. It was an answer to prayer for her and for us. A colleague was cultivating cactus as a tent-making job in one country. An expert botanist was consulted and shortly after that he was on the flight there to give the needed expert advice to an amateur botanist.

One of the practical things one can do as a sender is to provide practical assistance in an emergency or in a specific project requiring materials. Orphanages, orphans, natural catastrophes like floods, earthquakes and famines are some prime examples. Used stuff in good condition (like books, stationery, clothes, food-stuff) are just the things needed in some of these situations. Those who have plenty can bless those who are in want. I know of some ministries that collect and store good secondhand stuff in preparation for some foreseeable emergencies – and these are happening in greater regularity than ever.

### 7. Exercise diligence

One of my duties is to check mail for our workers in closed countries. I act as their censorship board! This takes time and diligence. Some mail has to be hand carried, and if there is no one visiting them, I will summarise the messages and email to them.

Last year, one of our workers told me he needed an air-conditioner for his work. He said he was meeting some believers discreetly and he didn't want the singing to be a cause of complaint by the neighbours. An air-conditioner contains as well as shuts out noise. I told him I would like to help. The day after my return home, an email came from a colleague in the USA who out of the blue felt the need to send me US$2000 for ministry use. I had the joy of informing our worker and the donor about how the Lord matched the need and the gift, all in a day's work!

### 8. Go on a trip

Take a mission trip. Go and visit the people your church has sent and you have been supporting. Gain firsthand knowledge for yourself. Smell the air, taste the food, feel their burden, talk with their contacts and friends, suffer the inconveniences, pray with the believers, do a bit of sightseeing to understand the local culture and beauty. You will return home motivated to continue in your supporting role. Visits like this always bring encouragement to the missionaries.

## 9. Employ all communication tools to stay in contact

Electronic communication is one of the greatest tools God has given us to do a better and more effective job in missions. Use email, letters, cards, phone, fax to keep in touch with those on the field. Be informed about security issues in some countries. Mind your religious language and jargon when talking on the phone or emailing. Watch out for religious 'trigger' words that will draw unnecessary attention to the work and the worker. If unsure, refrain from communicating until you have clarification.

Be considerate in sending email. It is only courteous to ask before you forward them junk email attachments. We are recipients of junk mail from well-intentioned friends who never bother to ask if we want it in the first place. Some days, I get so much junk devotional and inspirational email messages that I do not know what to do except to trash them. I don't know why some people feel it is their duty to forward junk email. Please, if you are tempted, ask the recipient first before you do so. This is common courtesy. When you get a request for help, don't pass it on to someone else when you can do it yourself. Otherwise your sincerity is held in question.

## 10. Show loyalty to missionaries

Remember, missionaries are human. After years of stress and hard work, it is not uncommon to find them burnt out physically and wounded emotionally.

Some supporters are not very good at handling missionaries in trouble. Instead of providing the badly needed pastoral care and love, insensitive supporters (usually representatives of the missions committee) question, make judgement, become critical and may even go to the extreme of inflicting more hurt on the already wounded missionaries. Show loyalty by being their advocate. Speak out for them, and in defence of them, if necessary.

When they return home for a break, whether burnt out or not, don't overload them with ministry, unless they are asking for it. Usually, they just need a break – and I mean a real break. Send them on a package holiday so they can be on their own. Sleep is restorative, and so is proper food. Arrange accommodation, get a church member to provide transport. One of the easiest ways is to provide a nice meal (if you can't cook, take them out), or if your home is available, practise hospitality. Let's honour them like God would his servants.

Here is my parting shot. When you have the opportunity, write down some specific ways you want to be involved. You may want to consult the missions committee in your church about your offer of help. If there is no missions committee, start one!

While frontline missions may be long-term or short-term, serving as a sender or a supporter can be for as long as you want. In fact, the longer, the better. Your reward is in heaven.

# PART THREE

*Gone!*

# Chapter Twelve

# Start them young!

'He called a little child …'

(Mt. 18:2, NIV)

The disciples were at it again; it wasn't the first or the only time. They were arguing among themselves over the question 'Who is the greatest in the kingdom of heaven?'

(Mt. 18:1, NIV)

I thought the answer was obvious. There, standing among them was THE GREATEST – Jesus. And yet they could miss it completely. It just goes to show that we, like the disciples, can be so cross-eyed when we are absorbed in our small ambition, jostling for a place of significance, that we completely overlook the Person who really matters. Yet, the Lord was so gracious in his response; he used a child to drive home a very important point about being great – the way God sees it!

In my last book, I shared that God wants to use young people. Since then, my outlook in missions has expanded to include children. I am convinced that God also wants to use *children* in missions.

I have long wondered why children in church are taught everything in Christian education – lessons from David and Goliath, Joshua and Caleb, so on and so forth, but are not taught about missions. I don't read Jesus categorically saying only adults can be used in missions, and yet little is being done to get children involved in missions. The Great Commission is given to all, without exception. Granted children may be too young to go into so-called 'full-time' ministry, but surely it is never too early to get them started.

Several years ago, Jennifer came to me sharing her vision to mobilise children into missions. Jennifer also happens to be my sister who was instrumental in paving the way for me to become a Christian in 1971. Specifically, the idea was to impart the missions vision to children between nine and twelve years of age – children in their upper primary education.

How relevant and timely this aspect of ministry was became obvious pretty quickly. Shortly after its inception, invitations from churches came fast and furious. A small team was recruited, equipped with materials, backdrops, puppets, mime, games and rope tricks, and hit the road running, sharing the vision in school chapels and in churches. We found a real niche in this ministry.

Next, the Kids Plus Club was started. In no time, several hundred kids signed up as Kids Plus Club members. Membership has its privileges! Members received regular comics and newsletters. Quarterly events are organised to nurture and sustain missions interest.

One day Jennifer, having returned from an exciting trip to India, hit upon the idea of taking Kids Plus members on a missions exposure trip to India. This would be a true expression of what we had been trying to bring across to the children. We weighed the pluses and the minuses. We had loads of questions and doubts. Would churches and parents be happy to release their children for this? Would we be criticised for prematurely exposing young children to a very different (and difficult) situation? What about safety? Were we taking unnecessary risks? We had more questions than answers.

We contacted OM India about this and promptly received an enthusiastic welcome for such a group to visit. The facilities and the Hyderabad centre were ideally suited for this purpose. The proximity of the practical ministries flowing out of the centre to the surrounding areas was an advantage. They were conveniently close and safe enough for the children to travel to and participate in. The couple responsible for pastoral care, Marcus and Ammana Chacko, had volunteered to host the group. It didn't take us long to decide to take the plunge.

To our amazement, almost thirty kids signed up, plus nine adults, including some mothers. Jennifer would be the overall coordinator. My family also signed up. Our children, Justin and Marianne, were even more enthusiastic. Irene volunteered to bookkeep. As the only male adult, I volunteered to assist Jennifer, being responsible for anything and everything from shouting orders, getting the children to bed, making them eat (and not waste food), readying them for each programme, ensuring safety and most importantly, counting heads!

As a project, every kid was challenged to carry a large plastic 'China' bag of goodies for the children they would be interacting with. Each was to fill the bag with toys, stationery, goodies and clothes. One rule was that they must give their best, not junk and throwaways. We even told them to give away one of their favourite toys. Missions involves generosity and selflessness, and little acts like this helped to drive home this principle.

Meanwhile, we secured an agreement with the airline not to charge for the excess baggage. On the India side, the customs were contacted to waive any tax.

The night of departure at the airport was like a circus. Just imagine – families, extended families (grandma, grandpa, uncles and aunts, godparents, siblings), church friends, pastors, Sunday school superintendents, mission committees and more, all gathered there to bid farewell. After prayer and some last minute briefing, we boarded the plane. We were given the aft section. The hostesses were delighted with the kids. It was especially hilarious when the plane hit some turbulence. The kids would exclaim in unison with each roller-coaster movement of the plane. When the plane hit the tarmac at the Hyderabad international airport, the kids applauded, much to the chagrin of all on board.

At the immigration, faces lit up amongst the immigration officers on seeing the group of kids. This was probably the first time they had had such a group. The kids were briefed on what to say as the reason for the visit – 'educational exchange programme'. This was true in every way. True to their word, the custom officers simply waved us through despite the trolleys of 'China' bags and a mountain of luggage. Marcus and his team were on hand with two OM vehicles – a bus and a large van, to whiz us to the base in Secunderabad, the twin city of Hyderabad.

The kids were accommodated in flats of two bed rooms each, with attached bathroom and toilet. Each room was equipped with a fridge, heater for water and a pantry. It was adequate and comfortable. Weather-wise, being in December, it was nice and cool in the evenings and mornings. It was also a lull period in bookings and so we had the luxury of having the entire base to ourselves. It was 1.00 a.m. when the kids hit the sack; 3.00 a.m. Singapore time!

At 6.00 a.m., with barely five hours of sleep, I was woken up by a commotion – all the kids were already up and about, enjoying the crisp and cool morning air. Some kids said, 'Uncle Rodney, it's so nice and refreshing, like natural air-conditioning.' With only a short time to sleep I knew they would not last the full day ahead. But what could I do; nothing was going to stop childlike enthusiasm in a new place, a new country.

After breakfast, Marcus and Ammana gave the group some information about India and the programme we were going to have for the next six days. Meanwhile, I set about organising a game scheduled for the afternoon that would involve group effort in looking for clues and exploring the sprawling 11-acre OM Hyderabad base.

Located in the base is the big warehouse of books belonging to OM Books, the largest Christian book distributor in India. From this warehouse, three tonnes of books are shipped out every day. There is also the large OM Books retail outlet. Next to it is the OM India HQ block, housing the administrative offices that support the more than one thousand workers; the adjacent annexe is the William Carey Library and auditorium that could sit 600, and several classrooms for 40 students. There is a large dining hall for 300 diners, a stone throw away from the dormitories and flats that could accommodate 300. Two pool-size wells supply water to the base. The Good Shepherd Ministry, catering to the medical and educational needs of the surrounding villages and slums, has a clinic in the base, next to a chapel for the Telegu (state language) church that doubles up as a meeting hall. The rest of the base is used for some subsidiary farming. Several small fields offer space for recreation. The base is completely walled up with a road running in the middle, lined with coconut trees. It was indeed a haven for the kids, as it is for others who use

the base for retreat, conference, or study. With such a setting, it was not difficult for the kids to spend the entire
afternoon hunting for clues and exploring the facilities.

The first taste of ministry was the visit to more than
ten Indian homes. We wanted the kids to experience
what an Indian home was like and how people lived. To
avoid overwhelming the Indian hosts with such a big
group, we broke up into smaller groups and dropped in
at short notice. Questions were asked and blessings were
prayed for in each home. Ten kids were involved in a
Children's Club programme in one home and all of them
had a great time of learning. As we walked, we came
across makeshift pavement-dwellers. Home for them
was a mud wall, some plastic sheets and wooden frames
to provide the little privacy that was badly needed. For
illumination, only a naked candle flame was used. Many
children looked pitifully poor but were happy to pose
with the kids. The kids were quick in sharing the ever-
ready goodies in their backpacks. What amazed me was
the immediate rapport between the kids, regardless of
their status. The smiles and giggles softened an otherwise harsh dark night.

How do you feed kids for seven days who were used
to a diet of Chinese and western fast foods? With difficulty! Despite the special effort by the fabulous cooks to
moderate the spiciness of Indian food, most of the kids
were not used to it. When children do not want to eat,
they won't! We had to modify the standard fare of curry,
veg and spicy meats with bread, jam, noodles and fried
food. We even organised an evening meal at the dimly lit
Nanking Chinese Restaurant. After several days of
Indian food, the kids never tasted yummier fried rice
and fried chicken. We were not prepared to face their
parents when we returned with unhealthy looking and
starved kids!

Talking about parents – one would expect parents from a relatively affluent society to be reluctant, careful and overly concerned about their children going on this trip. To our surprise, nothing like this happened. Parents were more than delighted to release their children for a week in India with the happy expectation that their children would return enriched and more compassionate from the experience. Email was set up for them and nightly pleasantries and assurances were exchanged between the kids in Secunderabad and parents in Singapore.

The second day proved to be a significant outing for the kids and adults. An entire morning was spent visiting the Good Shepherd Ministry in the slums located on the other side of the airport runway. This ministry was started by OM to provide help and opportunities among the poor. The slums we went to were not the worst. They were quite livable. But then, livability is relative! A moderate slum was still a great shock to the kids who had never seen anything like it in their life.

During the morning, we would be interacting with the school started by the GSM. The students totalled around two hundred. The school building was an educational shock for the kids. There was only one zinc shed. What was the size of a normal classroom for 30 children in Singapore housed 200+ in the slum. Classrooms – or rather, class corners - had no furniture. Everyone sat and worked on the floor. The children were in some sort of uniform, with most barefoot. Their discipline was impressive. Just imagine row after row of bright-eyed, smiling children with gleaming teeth. They were raring to have an enjoyable time with the kids. The kids presented a musical item, a puppet show and a group song. Jennifer told a simple story. Then it was the school children's turn. And their enthusiasm nearly brought the roof down. They responded with songs in Telugu and Hindi, and could they sing! No child was missed when bags of sweets were handed out.

After the school visit, we split into three groups to visit the slum-dwellers. There are many types of slums in India. The one we had chosen for the kids to visit was not too bad – meaning, there would not be roads, but at least there were gravel paths. Some houses had four proper walls while most were makeshift. Toilets were just holes in the ground with four sticks and a gunny sack suspended to provide privacy. There was no such luxury as piped-in water in the homes but at least there were communal water points. Not only were the slums a habitat for human beings, there were heaps of rubbish, dogs, cows, bullocks, buffaloes, goats, cats, chickens, pigs, trucks, bicycles, motorcycles, auto-rickshaws, cars and pickups crowding into the little space available. There were a few shops – just four pieces of wood, 1 m by 2 m in size – selling basic local necessities like soap bars, candles, matches and little else.

As we walked, the school children followed along happily. We visited an old woman who turned out to be a believer. There was a sad expression on her face and she asked us for prayer. She showed us her broken lower arm. It had been broken for some time but she simply could not afford to get it fixed; it was left dangling. Such was the harsh reality. The kids, one could see, were feeling sorry for her, and for the many things they saw and people they met that day.

At the close of the day, we gave the kids an opportunity to express their feelings and impressions. Every single one, from the oldest down to the youngest, said that they would not complain again about what they had at home. Some were visibly moved. It was not difficult to see the compassion on their faces.

Another thing that impressed the kids were the people. They were everywhere! India is crowded. It seemed like every available space and corner was used up and occupied by people. It was impossible to miss those who live in abject poverty. But the picture would not be complete if we didn't mention the middle-class, who comprised a good part of the population.

One afternoon, the kids visited 'Paradise'. This is not a joke but the name of a shopping area, and therefore the busier section of Hyderabad. It is packed with shops and restaurants – and people, of course. Loaded with some cash from their parents to buy some souvenirs to bring home, the kids shopped at the handicraft centre and the department store. On seeing the presence of so many foreign children, the manager of the store invited the kids to sing in the public address system. Meixi, one of the older Kids Plus girls, obliged with a Christmas carol 'Joy to the World.' How about that!

Sightseeing was also part of the educational exposure. The 800-year-old Golconda Fort was a lesson in history itself. The hike up – almost four hundred steep steps – was a challenge, but all made it. What impressed us most was that the fort took 62 years to build – as long as a lifetime! Thereafter, we visited the Gandipet Dam – 6,300 feet long! The contrast between water on one side and dry land on the other was spectacular. The kids also visited the Science Museum and Charminar (char = four, and minar = minarets), the Muslim section of Hyderabad. The traffic around the city tower was impossible for pedestrians to cut through. The traffic police came to our rescue; several of them stopped the traffic flow to allow the kids to cross. That's service for you!

While dawn and dusk were cool, the afternoon sun was relentlessly hot, and the climate, dry. One should not underestimate the assault on all the senses from the heat, the dust, the noise and the crowd. The dryness resulted in some cracked lips among the children. Lip-salve and Vaseline came in handy. Otherwise, we were spared from ailments, unless you consider homesick-ness an ailment. Irene and I, being the only couple, doubled up as team parents. One or two slept in our room with the lights on as a consolation for missing their parents at home.

The traffic and the driving in India was an 'edutain-ment'. One of the two vehicles assigned to us was actu-ally a good size ambulance. Noise is not a constraint in India – anytime of the day and night. On the back of many trucks and buses was painted this sign – 'Please Sound Horn'. So everyone obliged. There was much hilarity when the driver of the ambulance (that doubled up as our bus) whizzed through the busy traffic with the siren on. An Indian colleague told of an accident that took place between two vehicles – it could have been avoided if one sounded the horn, said the other driver! Small vehicles, like motorcycles and auto-rickshaws (three-wheelers that could carry as many as eight pas-sengers in a squeeze), use foghorns – yes, the same ones used by 50,000 ton ships. At least their sound was intim-idating even if their size was not. One kid commented that the driving was like arcade racing, except scarier.

One morning, after a visit to the local fresh food mar-ket, Marcus, our perfect host, hailed eight auto-rick-shaws to take the entire entourage back to the base, a distance of 5 kms. With five to each auto-rickshaw, we boarded not expecting anything special. Before we knew it, the auto-rickshaws were speeding down the village roads at full throttle. It became an impromptu road race, with 40 kids and adults screaming all the way. It turned out to be the most exhilarating and exciting incident of the entire week. It was not every day that the auto-rick-shaw wallahs had such an excited group of foreign kids as passengers. They were only too happy to oblige with their driving skills. At the end of the ride, they even requested a group photo!

Interaction with Indian children came in the form of an afternoon of fun and games – where winning was not everything, but playing was. In fact, the team that came in last received the loudest cheer. Prizes were given to all teams and Christmas gifts were distributed.

On Sunday, Lily Tan, one of the mothers, led a group of children in a short program at the high Anglican church in the city. Jennifer led the second group to a Brethren Assembly, while Irene led the third group to the Telegu Church. The children enjoyed the opportunity to participate and discovered some new and different ways things were done. Many were entertained by the tambla – like an Indian bongo drum. Church members had enjoyed the visit of the children – kind and positive comments were received about the kids.

On our final morning, half the kids went to an Anglican school for a programme. About a thousand primary school students sat on the gravel ground while the kids presented a half-hour programme. At another school, the kids also presented a drama and puppet item at the assembly. The school had an autistic class and it was indeed a special experience to interact with them. One autistic boy had the ability to figure out the day of the week as quickly as we were able to tell him our date of birth!

It didn't take much to correctly guess that when the time came for the kids to leave, every single one of them expressed reluctance. They were already asking when we were planning a return visit.

What impact did the week have on the kids? Bryan Yu wrote about the impact on his eating habit, '*I learned not* to waste food because there are many who don't have enough.' Ailene Tan had this to say about gratitude: '*God taught me to be thankful for what I have and not to take things for granted in Singapore.*' Justin Hui was touched by the poverty: '*I saw how poor people live and I understand how they feel.*' Ng MeiXi drew an object lesson on educational contentment: '*The slums school of 220 students occupying a space the size of my classroom, for 40, and still we complain!*'

Our host, Marcus, in his parting speech, had only good things to say to the kids: '*It is a short time, but a very sweet time. We are so amazed that you adjusted so well to the climate, environment and food. We are so surprised that all of you have not suffered culture shock. You look so cheerful. It's amazing to see children like you, so willing to give and share. This is a good way to build a foundation for young people in the future.*'

'A good way to build a foundation for young people in the future.' Marcus succinctly articulated our desire in getting kids involved in trips like this.

Was it worth the effort? Definitely. Did we see the desired result? Yes. We do not know what the long-term effect this has on the kids. A few years from now, who knows, some may volunteer for a longer term of missionary service. And who can tell if they will not attribute it to the seed that was sown in their young hearts during the week in Hyderabad!

# Chapter Thirteen

# An ordinary girl made good

'We have here only five loaves of bread and two fish'
– Disciples
'Bring them here to me'
– Jesus

(Mt. 14:17,18, NIV)

We were sitting at the Starbucks Café enjoying our lattes.
Of medium height, she looked ordinary for a
Singaporean. Her complexion would have been fair if
not for the past few years living at high altitude. As we
started talking, the drive she exuded and the passion she
expressed soon dispelled any thought of her ordinari-
ness.

Before joining OM, Jane (not her real name) ran her
own accounting firm. She majored in Mathematics at
university but realised earlier on that her nature was
more suited to be a social worker.

'I am highly motivated and practical,' Jane described
herself. 'And I think I am both task and relationship ori-
ented.' This sounded contradictory. How that was possible she had no idea, but she just knew. Her sense of opti-
mism and cheerfulness was infectious. 'I am also a simple

girl – in material and in philosophy,' Another contradiction? Colleagues and staff said she was serious with her work, but fun to work with at the same time. They knew it because they had seen her love for them.

So how did a mathematician turned accountant turned 'tent-maker' in Nepal end up in missions in the first place?

Jane became a Christian when she was fourteen years of age. At eighteen, she sensed God's calling for her into missions at a church missions conference. A desire was sparked in her heart to work in the third world. But the question uppermost on her mind was, where?

The answer came in 1997 at a Direction (missions) Camp run by OM. There, she heard about OM's need of a bookkeeper in Nepal. Although she had preferred a ministry rather than an administrative role, she did not mind as the position was on a part-time basis. The rest of the time could be used for ministry.

Like most Singaporeans from a Chinese family, she faced parental objection initially. But after the initial shock, her parents left the decision to her.

Upon arrival in Nepal, she did become the bookkeeper in the first year and she did get involved in the evangelistic work, just as she was promised. It was a good compromise that had worked out quite well. After the first year, she became the leader of the team of seven ladies. Leading a team involved planning duties, activities and seeing to each member's welfare and development. Some of the team members taught English to Nepalis, others helped out at children's centres, but all were involved in friendship evangelism – this involved befriending people, developing meaningful friendship and finding opportunities to share the gospel with them.

In the course of her ministry, Jane was requested by a Nepali co-worker to look after Dilu. Dilu, like many

Nepali women, was a single mother. Her husband was an alcoholic in the village and one time, in his drunken stupor, set his son on fire. Later he simply disappeared from the village. Like many Nepali women, Dilu was illiterate and unskilled. With a son to look after and without the resources to put him through school much less in a children's home, she was in desperate need. Jane's job was to provide the care, support and friendship that Dilu needed.

There was a sewing project run by another Christian outfit from which Dilu was able to learn some sewing skills. Having learned to sew, Dilu was still unemployed. To help her out, Jane forked out US$30 from her own pocket, bought some materials and some samples of handicrafts from the market and got Dilu to sew some replicas. When Dilu was done, Jane set out to sell some of the finished products – mainly Nepali coin pouches.

'Friends bought the finished products out of sympathy!' mused Jane. With the profit from the sale, she gave some to Dilu and the rest was used to purchase more materials to make more pouches. This private arrangement steadily grew and Dilu began to earn some income that she could live on.

Then an idea struck Jane.

'If I could do it for one lady,' thought Jane, 'why not for two?' So another woman was recruited. In the course of time, more were added to the number.

Having people buy the products didn't mean that the products were of a high quality, observed Jane. If the products were not of a high quality, the business would quickly fail. The goal was to improve on the quality – to bring them to a marketable and compatible standard with those that were already in the market. The challenge was to bring the business to a sustainable level in the long-term.

The handicraft business has since grown. After several years of experimenting and learning, the quality of the handicrafts is compatible and they are easily sold to NGOs, Christian organisations and some souvenir shops.

'Business prospered when we found a niche and a demand for the services or products,' said Jane, sounding like a business guru. The same principle may also be applied in the missions context – in that when the fundamental needs of people are met, ministry prospers.

Today, there are 20 women working at the craft centre. 'The centre symbolises hope,' she declared. 'I want to bring hope to those women.' This group of women came from terrible backgrounds. Some are single mothers who had been physically abused by their husbands while others had run away to escape ill-treatment, only to discover they had nowhere to turn. There are also widows among them. Some were ex-prostitutes. Many have children but were without resources to see them grow like normal kids. All are genuinely appreciative of the employment that the centre provides.

Thus began what has now become a small and self-sustained cottage industry.

'My strategy is simple,' Jane admitted, 'what we make must be sold; products must be moved. They are not allowed to accumulate.' This way, the business is solvent financially. From selling to sympathetic friends and local contacts, the market is being expanded. The cheaper prices and better quality mean they have been able to carve a niche in the market. The main worry is that products like these last a long time and people don't think of replacing them so quickly.

And all this started because of a misunderstanding.

'At that time,' Jane told the story, 'my Nepali was limited.' When Dilu shared a dream she had with her, she misunderstood it as God wanting Dilu to learn to sew. Later, when her Nepali was better, she finally understood that Dilu was trying to tell her that the dream she had was about God using her to start a sewing ministry! Even in a misunderstanding, God worked.

Later, Jane was faced with a dilemma with Dilu, who had shown no improvement in her sewing skills. She simply could not upgrade. In the end, Jane helped her set up a small restaurant. Unfortunately, she started selling cheroot and alcohol, the same items that had nearly destroyed her life earlier on. With Dilu, as with all the women under her charge, Jane learned women-management skills!

Some time later, a short-term team visited Nepal. Joe, one of the team members, after learning what Jane was doing, suggested to her the idea of making and selling soap. Joe informed her that JoJo, his wife, was very knowledgeable and might be able to help.

'I shelved the idea as soon as I heard it,' Jane said. Busyness in the ministry and the constant attention given to the handicraft centre was occupying much of her time and energy. Also, her (expiring) visa situation was looming at the back of her mind. After four years, she was still on an annual, renewable student visa. This did not give stability and assurance of continuity. A way must be found to obtain a longer term business visa to enable her to remain.

On the next visit to the immigration office, her fears were confirmed. Foreigners were not given business visas for handicraft and carpet industries. These are uniquely Nepali in nature, she was told. As a last resort, Jane suggested to the immigration officer – how about hand-made soap? To her surprise, the answer was affirmative. The manufacture of soap is relatively unknown in Nepal. The idea of the transfer of this technology to

Nepal was welcomed. A five-year business visa, renewable every year, was issued to her. The next thing for her to do was to start the soap business! What began as an idea had to be followed up with some concrete plans.

'I started finding out how to make soap, fast!" Jane exclaimed. On a trip to Britain for a leadership course in the seaside retreat centre in Wales, she bought a book on how to make soap. She read and soaked up everything on this subject. She learned everything needed to be learned about soap-making. She wanted to be practical too. Her first attempt at making soap was great in presentation but failed miserably in quality. She also corresponded with Robert, a Singaporean businessman, who was helpful with his advice and input.

'When I returned to Kathmandu, I experimented in earnest,' giggled Jane. 'At first, I thought there were only two types of soap: solid bar and liquid. As I found out more, the information forever changed the way I buy soap.'

Seldom do we think about soap as a load of chemicals, but it is. She gave this information: 'Each day we apply a whole host of chemicals on to our skin. No wonder some people, adults as well as children are allergic to soap!' Chemicals are used in commercial soap to give it colour, lather, smell and hardness.

'I learned,' volunteered Jane, 'that most commercial soap is made with animal fat. I do not fancy applying lard on to my face!'

As a result of her study, research and experiment, she came up with a formula that is 100 per cent natural. Her soap is made from a mixture of vegetable and essential oils, which are extracts from flowers.

When asked how her soap is made, she refused to disclose her trade secret except for these general steps – first, you mix oils and alkaline at the right temperature.

Then you enhance the soap with a combination of oil and essential addictives. Stir until the mixture thickens. Then, pour it into moulds. Next comes the insulation of the moulds. When the soap is hardened, hand cut it. It is then cured for as long as three weeks. Finally, the soap is trimmed by hand. And by hand each piece is individually wrapped. The labels are self-printed and hand-cut. 'Believe me,' Jane concluded, 'refining the technique and process took time!'

It was a year of trial and error. Commercial and large-scale soap product use machines but Jane only had simple womenfolk to do the job.

Like the handicraft centre, the soap venture provided employment for other women in need. All ingredients and materials used are natural. The uniqueness is that no preservatives are used. 'From the start to the finish,' she declared, 'everything is hand-made.'

For this enterprise, Jane rented a three-storey building. The factory is on the first floor, the office on the second and her accommodation is on the third. From a small group of women workers, the little factory now employs 27 women and five men. The men make purchases, including the import of ingredients from overseas. Sales are also improving, with a steady and increasing demand coming from Singapore and other countries. The contacts are made each time she visits home.

What is it like running two businesses? Her reply underlined the ethos: 'We are like a big family. We talk about family matters, sing and talk some more in the course of our work.' The women are especially touched when Jane provides the personal care for them.

What are some of the struggles that come with such work?

'People are still people,' sighed Jane. 'They backbite, they are unhappy even when I help.' It was disheartening at times. There was a deaf and dumb girl who accused her of not feeding her and of withholding her money. Another struggle is the difficulty in recruiting long-termers to work with her. Short-term volunteers provide only short-term assistance and relief. The culture is also a challenge.

'The Nepali culture is so laid-back. I am type A – the activist. None of my workers is type A!'

When a ministry is going well, the enemy counterattacks. Several articles in the local papers were written accusing her of proselytising. A rival, who had poached some of her workers, had also stolen her trade secret. This same person had orchestrated events that led to the reversal of her visa. A Nepali lawyer was engaged to deal with this situation while she waited for the outcome outside of Nepal. Not long after our meeting in Starbucks, the good news came that she had won the court case. She is preparing her return.

But what keeps her going?

Jane finds great satisfaction when she sees the quality of life improving among the women. It is a great encouragement for her to see single mothers now with the ability to buy food with their own money and send their children to schools. It is also good to see mothers and children putting on weight. This means they are getting the nutrition that they lacked before. Jane sees that God loves them practically.

But the greatest thrill is to see some coming to know the Lord. There is a lady who came to the Lord while working with her. She started sewing at the handicraft centre, but it soon became obvious that she couldn't sew. Another job was found for her – working as a maid. According to Jane, this lady has kept in contact and started bringing friends, and then her own sister, to the Lord. The chain effect is heart-warming.

In the future, Jane would like to see Nepali taking over the handicraft centre and the soap business. Her goal is to see both centres self-sufficient.

Her motivation is still to help more people find employment so that they may find dignity in their self-sufficiency and in so doing, find the Lord.

# Chapter Fourteen

# Pioneers wanted

What does a pioneer look like?

Talk of a pioneer and we think of names like David Livingston, William Carey, Hudson Taylor and C.T. Studd.

What does a modern pioneer look like? He is definitely not like the above. As a matter of fact, the modern pioneer looks just like you and me. Quite ordinary.

TS (name changed) is one such pioneer. He is quite young – early forties is not old! He doesn't look like a seasoned missionary but he is on his way to becoming one if he is not one already. What I am saying is that he doesn't look a bit like an old hand. On the contrary, TS is one of those endowed with a perpetual youthful look. He is married to LH and they have two young children.

He started his career as an accounts clerk in his hometown in Malaysia. After a short stint, he vowed not to be an accounts clerk for the rest of his life. 'I was just not cut out for it,' he lamented. So he tried his hands as a real estate agent. That lasted only six months. He figured that there was more to life than selling land and houses.

'I wanted to save souls,' said TS.

In 1979, as a single young man, he joined OM and served two years in Pakistan. OM was just pioneering in that country and he was destined to be part of the team. It was there in Pakistan that he received his life calling. TS recalled the call to prayer constantly blared out of the nearby mosques. It was as though the voice of God was calling to him and asking 'Did you hear?' – 'whom shall I send?' There and then he committed himself to this special work and began to cultivate a passion to see churches planted.

'Everything will be burnt,' reflected TS, referring to the test by fire that God will use to test our work. 'But not when we are building his kingdom in the lives of people.'

Returning from Pakistan, TS enrolled in the Singapore Bible College. In three years, he finished his course and found a job as a pastor in Malaysia. In 1986, he spent six months on the ship MV Doulos. Marriage came in 1990. His wife, LH, was a trained social worker. They met while studying at the Bible college.

Together, they returned to the Sind Province in the southern region of Pakistan. They chose this province because there was no church among a population of 50 million Sindhi people. Church planting was their goal.

TS's gifting as an entrepreneur became obvious as the ministry developed in the Sind Province. They started a computer centre, a library, typing classes and an English language centre. Soon after that, a sewing centre was also started, providing vocational training for men and women who were otherwise unskilled. A primary school, named The Way Primary School was founded and 80 students enrolled in the first year.

Time flew by and before they knew it, seven years whizzed by. Suddenly, without warning, TS was given one day to leave Pakistan. He was deported. Until this day, he is still not entirely sure of the reason or reasons for his deportation. His wife and family followed within the next two weeks.

In all the seven years, TS could claim only one convert. His dream and goal of a Sindhi church was never realised. Was there a feeling that all these years were wasted? If he was disappointed and discouraged by the lack of results, he did not show it. On the contrary he has reasons to rejoice. The one person who came to faith went on to be trained in a theological seminary. In turn, this person discipled five more young men. Of the five, three are in full-time ministry – attached to OM and another ministry. The fourth became a doctor and the last, a teacher. For several years, this core group of people has been able to send two persons to participate in the annual outreach programme that OM conducted.

What do you do when you have been kicked out of a situation with nowhere to go? It is not unusual to feel despair, to give up, to question God, get angry, or blame yourself and others. TS did none of these.

After a brief respite, TS was looking for an open door. The world is big and if one door is closed, there are dozens that are opened. With his experience and gifting, it was only a matter of time before a suitable placement was available to him and family.

'Our hearts were still burdened for the special group of unreached people,' said TS. After a year and a half of waiting, they found an open door.

Tajikistan!

Many Christians knew little about this new republic in the former Soviet Union. Christians were few and Christian workers, even fewer.

Ninety three per cent of Tajikistan is mountainous, making it one of the most beautiful countries in Central Asia. The temperature range – from a low of –10C in winter and a maximum of 40C in the heat of the summer – makes this place ideally livable. Built and developed by the Russians, the cities have the appearance of culture. Unfortunately, such development does not extend beyond the cities. The countryside is basic, simple, backward and perhaps even primitive. The country is generally poor. As a matter of fact, Tajikistan is the poorest country among the new republics.

This country of six million is more than 90 per cent Muslim but remains a secular state. However Islam is on the rise. When the country was first open in the early nineties there were only 16 mosques. Today, there are more than 2000 mosques dotting the country.

What does one do in such a country with little Christian activity? Where does one begin?

'As soon we got there, we discovered God was already at work,' reported TS. Many Christian workers had entered and were effectively serving the Tajik people. NGOs (non-government organisations) were registered to facilitate visa acquisition for workers. Projects were launched to meet the physical needs of the Tajiks. Emergency relief of food and clothing was given to the poor who had suffered from natural calamities and the civil war between 1992 and 1997.

TS went straight to work. He joined an NGO whose goal is to demonstrate the love of God through humanitarian work. One aspect of this is community development. The 12,000 people up in the mountainous region just north of the capital are targeted. The staff has been teaching mother/child health and hygiene care for the past five years. Discussion groups among women are going on in 11 villages. A micro-enterprise scheme is also available to help poor Tajiks with some form of livelihood. For instance, participants of the scheme get a donkey that will in turn bring in some income.

To the average person, Tajikistan seems as remote as Timbuktu. Is the country as isolated as it is land-locked? Accessibility by air, though better than it used to be, is still not as straightforward – one has to fly a roundabout route to get there. Telecommunications in some of the new republics seemed to have leapfrogged into the new century. In 1995, the NGO that TS is a member of started the first email service in the country, which turned out to be hugely successful. Presently, there are as many as eight email centres across the country providing free email services to 12,000 Tajiks, all major universities, government offices and other organisations. People queue up to use these services. In addition, computer classes are also offered.

Tajikistan, like many third world countries, believes that in order to stay connected and to keep pace with the outside world, as many of its people as possible should be encouraged to learn the English language. Some assume knowing English is a passport to career development. An English Language Centre was started with five English teachers working to provide high quality English classes. There is a waiting list of 200 people wishing to take the courses!

After several years of stability, TS launched into church planting work. Three teams were formed for this purpose. A literature ministry was also started. This involves the translation, printing, production and distribution of books in the local language. There is a Tajik lady whose job it is to sell Christian literature to the local bookshops. Not long after that, the team started producing Christian music tapes and videos in the local language.

When Tajikistan opened up more than ten years ago, there were only a handful of churches, mainly Russian.

'It is a joy to see one group of thirty to forty Tajik believers worshipping together,' said TS. There are

many small groups springing up in the capital
Dushanbe.

Stories of God working through dreams and visions
of Tajik people are common.

One lady testified that God revealed himself to her in
her dream no less than three times. First, she dreamt
about the giving of alms. The second time, she was
instructed to sacrifice a lamb. In her third dream, she
was walking down a path that was dark on both sides.
In front (she was able to determine later) was Jesus,
standing there inviting her to the bright side. After that,
she sought to find an explanation of her dreams.

This lady works in a chemist shop. One day, while
passing by her shop, one of the team members for some
strange reason felt an unquenchable thirst. Stepping
into the shop, she requested a glass of water. On accepting the water, she remarked that 'Jesus will not forget
the glass of water given to me.' She noticed a religious
book by the side of the hostess and before both knew it,
they were engaged in a meaningful conversation. The
team member quickly found out that this lady was
searching. The long and short of it is that this lady is
now a believer.

As individuals began to make the decision to follow
Jesus, TS, who by now was giving attention to the spiritual
development of the work, thought of a way to bring them
together to form a church. With the issue of security still an
unknown, the best way was to organise them into smaller,
cell groups. Thus, several groups were formed. Within a
year, one group saw its number doubled. Ten have been
baptised in the past two years. 'For those who were just
baptised, we immediately taught them how to preach,
never mind if they were still young in the faith,' said TS.

The small Tajik church that TS is leading sent its first
missionary-to-be for theological training in a Bible

school in Kyrgystan: Z (full name withheld) – only eighteen years of age.

'Z was one of a set of twins,' recounted TS. Her mother died when she was young. Her stepmother, who brought her up, mistreated her. She was sent to an 'internat', like a cross between an orphanage and boarding school. While there, she developed such a deep hatred towards her stepmother that she vowed she would kill her when she was old enough. When she turned sixteen, she was released from the 'internat'. Without friends and relatives, she was left with nowhere to go. She fell gravely ill with hepatitis and went to hospital. She was left to die there, and she almost did! It was while she was in hospital that a Russian Baptist lady visited her. Not only did Z become a believer, she was also healed of her sickness!

When she left the hospital, she still had nowhere to go. That was when she was introduced to the NGO female staff, one of whom has two daughters of her own of the same age. While staying with them temporarily and in an NGO halfway house, Z started going to the fellowship. Her spiritual desire grew just as her interest in the Bible increased. Her next step was baptism.

During her baptism classes, she began to work through issues in her life and her deep hatred for her stepmother surfaced. To cut a long story short, she made a decision to go back to her stepmother to ask for forgiveness. This was done, forgiveness was sought, and she got on with her life. For someone who had gone through so much hardship in life, the Lord surely has something beautiful in store.

When she returns from her training, Z, who has a burden for an unreached people group up in the Pamir Mountains bordering China, will be pioneering a work there. The small church will be adopting her as their worker and will send her out when the time is right. To think of a young church sending a young missionary is exciting indeed. It is a good and healthy start.

How does one plant a church in a place like Tajikistan?

Where there has never been an established Tajik church before, the foreign workers were the first resource.

'I made use of long-termers,' said TS. But what about the short-term workers? What do they do if they don't speak the language? 'They just sit and listen,' replied TS. 'This way they get to learn. When you show love, it does not matter if you don't know the language.'

With the team, the strategy is to spend the first six months to a year befriending Tajiks. Long-termers who know the language are able to build such relationships. When the ex-pats come together to fellowship and worship, all team members, whether long- or short-term, would invite Tajik friends along. Some come because they want to learn English, while others are attracted to the faith and testimony of the ex-pats.

The question invariably arose – where to meet when there was no church building available?

'We decided to start by holding it [the meeting] in a hotel,' said TS. Several reasons persuaded them to do it this way. 'Firstly, if our faith is worth anything,' he explained, 'it is worth testing it against any adversity, whether perceived or real.' Although it was not known if the authorities would object, it was better to do it openly and formally.

'Secondly,' continued TS, 'we wanted to lay the right foundation for future believers.' When there is no prototype you have to ask, what model does one want to leave? Another reason behind this move is to cultivate boldness. 'We do not want the believers to hide and feel insignificant right from the word go.' As it turned out, there was some intimidation from the KGB, but nothing serious.

Thirdly, in using the medium of English and Tajik, the meeting would attract the better educated. Using a hotel as the venue would be most appropriate.

Lastly, there was no model of a properly operating Tajik church to copy. In starting openly this group sets the pace and the example. Other groups who were more cautious would realise that it is all right to be out in the open.

Some may disagree with this approach, but so far, it has worked quite well.

On the negative side, they didn't know what problems and outcomes would arise out of this initiative. While holding the meetings in a hotel would attract the educated, it also attracted people on the fringe of society – like the odd rebel and misfit.

Now that the initial phase is over, and with increasing uncertainty over the freedom to practice religion, another approach is being adopted.

They now meet in smaller cell groups. For three times a month they meet in such groups, and on the fourth time, come together as a big group. At each meeting, the gospel is preached from the Bible. The advantages of this approach are many. It helps develop lay leadership very quickly. Even the newly baptised are taught to share from the word. It is a lot easier to extend mutual care towards one another. While centralisation will tax a small team, this approach spreads the load of responsibility. There is no need to employ a pastor and no need to buy a 'church' building. This way, the church comes to the neighbourhood. While this may raise questions, often what it does is arouse curiosity, which in turn is turned into witnessing opportunities. Even if the freedom to worship is held in question, smaller cell groups like these would survive should a crackdown take place.

Pioneering work is not without its struggles. For TS and LH, it was loneliness in Pakistan. In Tajikistan, it is the time, effort and energy in maintaining relationships with co-workers. There have been 'fights', admitted TS, but thankfully these fights do not break friendships. It takes maturity to work and walk in such a precarious environment. Then there is the demand on the family. Balancing time between the family, the work as a protocol officer, as the leader, ministry and church planting work, is just about impossible. It is no surprise that many get burnt out if the right rhythm is not maintained.

Just as struggles are part and parcel of pioneering work, so are the joys. 'What a joy it is to see lives changed,' said TS. 'To see others staying longer, staying focused and happy in their work.' But no joy can be compared to that of seeing the church started. In a few short years, from a handful of Tajik believers, the number has mushroomed to a total of around two thousand. TS is only too aware that his part is small compared to the work done by other groups.

TS and family are still in Tajikistan. His story has not ended yet, of course. As a Malaysian, and a Chinese, his heart is to challenge and mobilise the Chinese Church into missions. He has proven that it is possible. 'Often,' said TS, 'missions is associated with westerners.' And in places like South and Central Asia, westerners remind them (though unfairly) of the crusades in history, of imperialism and of loose morality as depicted in the media, which all serve to erect barriers to the gospel. As a fellow Asian and a Chinese Christian, often the response is in the form of disbelief – how can a Chinese be a Christian?! Seeing Chinese Christians does give them a new perspective on Christianity.

Asked if he could describe himself as a survivor and a pioneer, TS said he was more a dreamer, a futurist and a plodder. He has proven himself to be an entrepreneur, persuasive salesman, less a thinker than a doer. Are these the qualities of a pioneer? Maybe, maybe not.

He does have his negatives: 'I am not a detail person. I take things and people for granted. I can be insensitive and I can be pushy.'

We need people like TS and LH – people in missions who are in for the long haul. Keeping at it through thick and thin. Through fair weather and foul. Through good and ill. Through compliments and complaints . . . not unlike an older couple – the husband is sixty-seven and his wife, sixty-six – who are working with him in Tajikistan. They are retirees with experience in running a business. People with business experience are greatly needed in missions. Planning to 'retire'? What about going on missions on the last leg of your life? The benefits are out of this world.

(*Postscript – Recently, the first Tajik church was officially registered with the authorities. It was an historic moment!*)

# Chapter Fifteen

# Story of an immigrant

My one and only visit to the country of Iran took place in 1976, while on an overland trip from Holland to Singapore. At that time, I could not remember if there was an Iranian church. I did not get a chance to visit one nor meet Iranian Christians.

My first real experience of learning about the Iranian church was 21 years later when, for one full week, I listened to an Iranian speaking at an international conference. This pastor was a dynamic and authoritative preacher. His authority, I concluded, came from the persecution, the pressure and the willingness to risk his life for the sake of the gospel living and pastoring in Iran.

The next true Iranian believer I met was Michael.

I heard about Michael from Richard Beaumont, an Australian friend of mine. Richard and Michael initiated a work in Australia in '97 ministering to migrants. By all accounts, this ministry is meeting a vital need in reaching out to the minority and immigrant population. It was at an OM staff retreat in Melbourne that I got to meet Michael and his German wife, U (name withheld) and their two young sons.

Michael met his wife in India when they were both involved in the ministry among the Afghan refugees. As true and submissive OMers, they adhered to the social policy guidelines for couples who want to begin a meaningful relationship. Nothing came out of their contact in India though there was some interest. When Michael migrated to Australia, the correspondence continued. Two years later, when U visited Australia, they got engaged. Shortly after that, they were married in Germany.

Michael was apprehensive about U's parents' reception. Would her parents be willing to accept an Iranian as their son-in-law? To his relief and surprise, he faced no objection. As committed and mission-minded Christians themselves, U's parents had welcomed and accepted him. 'I was treated very well,' beamed Michael. In 1993, they returned to settle in Sydney, Australia.

Brought up in an Iranian family, Michael had no contact whatsoever with Iranian or ex-pat Christians. In 1978, he went to study in New Delhi, India. 'It was in the year 1984 that I heard the gospel for the first time on the radio,' recalled Michael. He had never come across a Christian radio programme before. His interest was easily aroused. In response to the invitation at the end of the radio program, he wrote in to request for a correspondence course. 'I saw the English Bible for the first time in India,' said Michael, 'I never knew the Bible existed. I thought it was lost in the olden time.' Having obtained a personal copy, he started reading it, and fell in love with Jesus.

What was it about Jesus that attracted him? 'Jesus practised what he taught,' he answered. As an Iranian, religion had little or no influence on his life. He had fasted and prayed, but no change had come to him. "Each time when I broke fast,' confessed he, 'I would be back to my old self.'

The verse that sealed his decision to follow Jesus was John 14:6: 'Jesus answered, "I am the way and the truth and the life. No one comes to the Father except through me."' Michael came to the conclusion that Jesus was a prophet and true prophets didn't tell lies. So he accepted Jesus, and that began a journey that saw his faith and his walk tested.

When his parents found out that he had become a Christian in India, they stopped sending him money for his studies. He found himself in financial trouble. To make ends meet, he would buy goods from India and sell them in Iran when he returned there for a visit. For his return trip to India, he would buy goods in Iran to sell in India. 'One time, I carried four suitcases of clothes overland through Pakistan to Iran to sell,' he laughed. Profits from this trade were used to cover his living expenses and school fees.

As a young Christian, he had to learn to trust the Lord to work on his behalf. One clear incident of God's overseeing his life was at the border crossing to Iran. He recalled: 'I was loaded with goods to trade. I was travelling together with two other Iranians. The customs officer on duty asked what we had in our suitcases. The two Iranians lied about what they had. One of them ended up having to pay 2,000 Iranian toman. This amount is not much now but it was a lot at that time. The other was taxed 3,000 toman. When my turn came, I told the truth. And I was told to pay 5,000. The next day was the New Year and the customs officer told us if we wanted to cross the border we had to come back before the border closed, otherwise we would be stuck for the next three days. While the other two went back to exchange money, I stayed to pray. When the two returned, all three of us went back to the same customs officer. The two guys paid up. Then the customs officer turned to me and said,

'You don't have to pay.' I crossed the border with much thanksgiving to the Lord!'

In 1985, he went back to Iran for his summer holiday. While in Teheran, Michael was longing for some fellowship with Christians, but was deterred by the unfriendly high walls churches built. In 1986, he was back again to Iran. This time, he had returned prepared – he was given an address and a telephone number. He was successful in his search for fellow Iranian Christians. 'That was my first time seeing the Persian Bible,' cried a delighted Michael. 'I bought a copy and listened to Christian songs in the Persian language, my mother tongue.

'My parents didn't take me seriously,' continued Michael. 'They thought I was given money to become a Christian, or that a Christian girl was behind my conversion.'

On one occasion, he ended up arguing with his parents, brothers and sisters. As a new believer, he could not understand their questions, let alone answer them. That night he could not sleep. Michael remembered: 'I felt discouraged and started complaining to Jesus. I wept until my pillow was wet from my tears. I complained to the Lord – Why did you send me alone to Iran when you sent your disciples two by two? Then I had a vivid dream. In my dream, I saw a vision of a bright light in the form of a man. Then I felt Jesus gripping my hand and saying to me – "You are not alone." When he left, I sat up, feeling a lot better!'

Michael left Iran to return to India to complete his studies. In 1988, he graduated with a PhD in Linguistics. Then he became a refugee, the reason being that he did not want to be a secret believer living in Iran. While living in Delhi, he came to know about OM and got involved in the team ministry. The team was engaged in work among the Afghans but Michael felt more needed to be done among Iranians. As a last resort he wrote to appeal to George Verwer, the founder of OM. In reply, George wrote to challenge Michael to do it himself.

That letter got him thinking. 'I am from the Middle East. I am Iranian,' he reasoned. 'Only westerners can be missionaries. Not me.' The more he thought about it, the more he wondered, 'but why not?' The excuse was a lame one. By then, Michael, as a refugee, was working with the UN and paid by the UN. Shortly after that, he decided to resign from his work with the UN to join OM, and began his ministry among the Afghans and Iranians. He started the correspondence course in Delhi and opened a school teaching English to the women. About eighty students enrolled in this school. Ex-pat OMers came to help out in teaching Afghan women English.

In 1991, he emigrated to Australia. At that time, the UN asked Canada and Australia to accept Iranian refugees, especially people with experience like Michael. To return to Iran as a Christian was deemed risky.

'At first, it was hard to settle in Australia,' admitted Michael. He hardly knew anyone and he was broke. He had to start everything from scratch. There were formalities that came with resident status, like arranging for his social security. That done, he went about helping the Iranian fellowship that had just started in Sydney. He enrolled at a Bible college. He was busy with theses to write. But the problem was the college fee. Michael knew every student had to pay, but he was broke. Believing God had wanted him to study, he continued attending classes. The faculty did not know what to do with him. Eventually, because of him, they started a scholarship fund. Christians started giving and thus his fees were paid. Staying outside the campus helped in reducing the expenses. Giving from U's supporters also helped. At the end of the two years in the Bible college, Michael and U rejoined OM in Australia.

How did the immigrant ministry start in Australia?

'I rejoined OM after school in 1997 in order to work in Central Asia,' Michael admitted, 'because I speak the language of Tajikistan.' As a matter of fact, he was in Germany to see if he could obtain a visa. However, many supporters did not have peace about this. The main reason was their concern for his safety in Tajikistan. At that time, Richard Beaumont, then OMA Director, counselled Michael to remain in Australia and to train others to go. That was the beginning of the immigrant ministry.

Setting up took some effort. The promotion of this new ministry, brochures and publicity also took time. They decided that the goal was to train the local churches in reaching out to the minority immigrants. Workers are recruited through personal contacts and friendship. The response from Australian churches has been encouraging.

A week-long programme has been designed offering training and a hands-on evangelism opportunity among the minority peoples in Australia. Training includes a good dose of classroom lectures and teaching on beliefs and practices, culture and mindset, and how to share the faith. The practical aspect includes street outreach, sharing with groups of new believers and visits to religious centres.

Australia, with its religious freedom and multi-minority society, is an ideal place for such a work. In Sydney, there are about five to six thousand Afghans, and the number is growing. There are as many as 25,000 Iranians and several thousand from Somali. Sydney has also become the centre for Arab immigrants, while Melbourne attracts the Turks. However, most second-generation children of immigrants, born in Australia, speak English, and very little of the mother tongue. Life in Australia for the immigrants is comfortable compared to where they have come from. There is certainly a lot more freedom in almost every way. To become a Christian is not difficult in that there is no restriction and Aussie rule is that you can basic-ally do what you feel is right.

To work among the minority immigrant groups, there is no need to learn another language apart from English. In reality, however, team members are encouraged to learn another language. Although the ministry started with short-termers who came for a year or so, it is now run by long-termers. There is a family who used to work in Kenya among the Somalis but are now in Sydney reaching out to the same people. A Korean family, a lady from Papua New Guinea and several other singles make up the rest of the team. The work has grown through the years.

Beside individual contact and follow up work, the team also staff a book table in the market – a local focal point where anyone is free to talk to any team member or browse through the books available in various lan-guages. An hour-long radio programme for Afghans is also broadcast in the city of Sydney. Church planting work continues in the midst of this. The team however has not lost its essential focus of presenting the good news of Jesus Christ. Testimonies of individuals and families turning to the Lord abound.

On one of the courses conducted in the Gold Coast, a team heard about an Afghan family who lived near the church where the course was held. But no one knew the address. The team prayed asking the Lord to grant them 'a divine appointment' with this family. One afternoon, a team member spotted a woman with a headscarf at the local shopping centre. The member went up to her and asked where she came from. 'Afghanistan,' replied the woman. After some exchange, the team member learned that this woman and her family were the same family they were looking for! The team leader was able to visit them and found them so hungry for friendship and for the gospel that he could tell them about Jesus and left them a *Jesus* video in the language they speak.

On one outreach in Sydney, the team would pray for divine appointments every time they went out to meet contacts. Michael related: 'I went to a grocery shop to buy a few things and when I came out I started distributing literature to a few immigrants standing near the shop. As soon as they found out what it was one of them held my hand and said that he wanted to talk to me. I asked him to follow me and when we were a distance away from the others, I asked him why. He said that he wanted to know more about Christianity.

'I wanted to give him a New Testament but I had no more with me. So I asked him to give me his phone number so that I could contact him. I discovered he was from another city and was in Sydney visiting friends. After obtaining his mobile number I told him to stay near the shop until I return with a New Testament and a *Jesus* video.

'By the time I got back, he was no longer there. I waited for sometime and then called him on his mobile. He said that he'd had to leave, and it would be better if I posted the things to him. This I did, and added other Christian literature in his mother tongue.

'One day he phoned to say that he would be visiting Sydney again and asked if we could meet. So I met him and took him to my place to talk some more. God had truly prepared his heart and he had only one question to ask me: 'How can I become a Christian?' So he prayed and accepted the Lord. When he was leaving he said next time he comes to Sydney he wants his flat-mate to come along, because he is interested too."

Another time, another team member reported: 'I was walking in a suburb when I saw a group of immigrants in a pub. I started praying for them in my heart and later asked our prayer partners to also pray for them. One day I had a call from A who said that he wanted to meet me. When I met him he said that one day he was in a pub (the same pub) and suddenly he felt something telling him, 'what are you doing here, your people are in pain and you are wasting your money here.' He left the pub and went to a grocery shop and bought a Persian newspaper. In this paper he saw our advertisement offering a New Testament in his language, obtainable from a Christian bookshop in the city. He went to that bookshop and got our literature. Through the postal address and a phone number contained in the literature, he made contact with me. So we talked for two hours in the park. He accepted the Lord and now we meet regularly.'

These stories prove the readiness and hunger in the lives of many immigrants. There are many more. The ministry is truly vital as a link for the immigrants to find the Saviour.

Heavy on Michael's heart is the salvation of his family.

'My parents are still in Iran and doing very well,' shared Michael. His father visited him in Australia not long ago. He found out that his father had been listening to Christian radio for two years and liked the Bible that Michael gave him. Everything in this Book is good, the father had said, and he had questioned why people were not allowed to read it back in Iran. In Iran, there are few Bibles and no bookshops. Michael then took the opportunity to share the gospel with him, and to his amazement, his father accepted Jesus. Not only had he the joy of praying with his father, he later baptised him!

Michael's mother is not a believer yet, neither are his siblings of two brothers and five sisters. Their misconception about Christians still runs deep. In Iran, only Armenians are Christians, and many Armenians live in immorality. For Michael to become a Christian is a reflection on the family's failure in his upbringing.

'My mother saw me and said "my son is better than before."' he testified. Once upon a time, his life and values were different – money was a big factor.

'But praise the Lord, he found me and I found him,' smiled Michael. 'Otherwise, I would still be lost.'

# Chapter Sixteen

# Love wins the day

In 1993, after my first visit, I wrote about this country:

- Half the population of 8+ million are below fifteen years of age
- Lowest workforce in the world
- Highest number of amputees in the world who lost their limbs to landmines
- An estimated 10 million landmines are still unaccounted for and probably untraceable – because many were made of plastic and therefore floatable during the monsoon
- One of the 30 least evangelised countries in the world
- Aid in the north-western region averages US$16 per month per person, elsewhere it is US$2
- Non-government organisations' projects total 900
- Vehicle theft in the capital is one of the highest in the world
- There is a book famine. There are few or no children's books
- The only country in the world with two ruling prime ministers with two police forces
- Highest agricultural share of GNP (Gross National Product) in Asia

- It has a language with the most letters in the alphabet – 72
- Worst genocide in percentage of population – more than one third of 8 million were slaughtered and killed
- World's largest single group of religious buildings found at Angkor Wat and Angkor Thom, which includes more than 600 Hindu temples.

If your guess is that this country is Cambodia, you are correct. The suffering and recent history of this country defies logic.

Sweeping changes have taken place since I wrote the above. The changes are positive: less random shooting, more political stability, increased engagement with neighbouring countries, economic growth, visible signs of increasing wealth, tourism – and positive signs of church growth, implying relative freedom in the practice of religion.

While the eighties and nineties saw almost an entire generation traumatised by the genocide of the late seventies – it was extremely hard to find anyone who did not have someone in the family killed during the Pol Pot regime – the twenty-first century is witnessing a new generation made up of 'damaged' and dysfunctional children. No where else in my extensive travel have I found so much sin committed by the human race, and against children in particular!

Child sexual abuse and physical abuse, paedophilia, child prostitution (one third of all prostitutes), slavery, child abandonment and pornography are the order of the day. Presently, as many as 200,000 of the population is HIV infected. This is a conservative estimate. Several thousand babies are born with HIV every year. Present figures of discovery number 14,000 every month! This is like a powder keg ready to explode in the near future.

One evening, I had dinner with Craig, a Kiwi, and his Cambodian wife, Nay (raised in NZ), and a small group of friends in the wooden structure they called home, right in the middle of a slum on the outskirts of Phnom Penh. Craig and Nay have been living among the poor for several years and their ministry is among the Aids victims. They partner with local churches, and through them, seek to provide the help and support to no less than 400 families with members who are HIV positive. Next door, Craig told us, lives a family whose father is going to die of Aids at any time. Their hope and prayer is that the love of Christ may shine through an otherwise hopeless situation.

In the midst of such human misery, a ray of hope is shining through the numerous humanitarian efforts by Christian churches and NGOs. Orphanages, rehabilitation centres, healthcare programmes, vocational training centres, clinics, schools, computer training centres, agricultural projects, aid and development initiatives have all been started to meet the need of rebuilding lives and society.

Li Diang and Carol were two dental nurses who had served on the MV Doulos after responding to the call of missions. After their two-year stint on board, they enrolled in a local Bible college in Singapore. As with many who had served a term in missions with OM, they were hooked. When college ended, they were duly recruited by the Methodist church to be involved in setting up a centre for children in Cambodia.

Located an hour's drive outside of Phnom Penh, the centre is a spanking new, brightly painted complex in an otherwise dull and monotonous landscape of partly swamps, partly flat paddyfields. The complex houses more than one hundred children of all ages. There is a multi-purpose hall, a dining hall, a playing field, class-rooms, computer room, music room, a clinic equipped with a dental chair, prayer room, chapel, dormitories for boys and girls, staff quarters, a mini farm that contains a chicken coop, a cow, pigs, and a vegetable patch. The mini farm provides a supplement to the daily diet of basic nourishment for the children and an experiment to teach the children about care and responsibility.

When I arrived, the boys and girls were hard at work scrubbing the dormitories, supervised by several sets of parents and families.

'We have divided the group into families,' said Li Diang. The idea was to create a family environment for the children and to encourage the Khmer staff raising the children. Children of school-going age are sent to the nearby Khmer school. There is a degree of goodwill with the school.

'We receive short-term hands-on teams regularly,' Li Diang explained. Last year, a team concentrated on repairing and sprucing up the village school. Now, the English-speaking staff of the centre have an exchange arrangement to teach English at the school.

A pair of six-year-old twins were playing happily near us. With their brown hair, it was obvious they were not pure Khmer. Li Diang informed me that at first they did not want to stay. One night, they ran away. But because the gravel road out of the centre leading to the main road was several kilometres away, it was not long before some farmers noticed them. The farmers knew straight away that they had come from the centre, and promptly delivered them back. 'Now,' said Li Diang, 'they are so happy here they don't want to leave!'

It is not unusual to receive children referred to by the government department handling abandoned children.

Not long ago, Li Diang was called to Phnom Penh to consider yet another boy. When she got there, she was shown two children – a brother and a sister – eleven and eight. The girl was already HIV positive. The boy looked miserable – he had an ugly, open wound festering on his leg. When asked, he said he was bitten by a dog. As the sister was taken care of by another NGO, Li Diang brought the boy home to the centre.

When they arrived, the boy was served a plate of steaming white rice and a bowl of hot soup. At first, he simply sat there and stared at the food. Then he started crying. He told Li Diang that he had never been given any food like this. In all his life, he had either to beg or to work for his food. The rice he had had always been cold, and made palatable only by adding some salt. Now, several weeks later, he was happily living in the centre and participating in the programmes.

'It is heartbreaking having to hear all sorts of stories,' admitted Li Diang. I could see why it was not difficult to feel the compassion and the love for the children when you had listened to the incredible journeys some had taken to get this far in life. The pain and suffering of some are several times worst than a normal average adult. How children of eight or ten years of age were made to endure the things they did is just unthinkable, and yet, there are thousands who are still trapped in this deadly cycle.

One common story is that caused by abandonment. Some of these children were simply abandoned by parents who either did not want them or were too desperate themselves. They were left to fend for themselves. Some survived on their own while others came under the control of syndicates. I heard the stories of several who had wandered into neighbouring Thailand and Vietnam to beg on behalf of a particular syndicate. How they came into the care of these NGOs is nothing short of miraculous.

Jung Young and Ki Young, both Korean ladies with OM, are also involved in children's ministries. In their case, with many more years of experience, the care and development of the children is ongoing. Whether or not one agrees with the approach to children's ministry, it involves long-term effort and commitment. It is easy to theorise about the pros and cons, to argue and debate over a method, but compassion does not come cheap. It is costly!

Their Korean supporters provided a Hyundai second-hand bus that was converted into a mobile clinic. Every week, the bus would make its rounds, providing basic healthcare to the surrounding areas.

At one centre, the several packs of goodies we brought for the 25 kids were eaten in record time. Some who were more careful, kept their portion. Several kids were clinging to us. This just showed how starved they were for affection and attention. I salute the staff for being there twenty-four hours a day providing that which is desperately needed.

At another children centre, Anba, a former OMer who was instrumental in establishing a holistic ministry, reported that two boys had run away to watch the Boat Festival. The rest of the children prayed for them, but they failed to return that night, and the following day. One was eleven and the other was six. One month later, Anba informed me that the two boys took a taxi all the way to the Thai border, about 400 kms distance, in their pursuit of freedom. They were promptly caught and brought back to Phnom Penh. It is the practice of the NGO not to accept again children who have run away.

'But,' smiled Anba, with a twinkle in his eyes, 'our Khmer staff will likely welcome them back.' Love wins the day.

This kind of work is not without heartache and disappointment. In a short period of time, I heard of five NGOs that had suffered some split or division, perhaps due to disagreement, personality, style of ministry or leadership. It could even be due to cross-cultural factors or the nature of the work. People were hurt and as a result, the work suffered a setback. Tiredness, emotional and physical burnout are the order of the day in such a demanding and exacting ministry.

Security, or the lack of it, is another area of concern. Theft and robbery are rampant. One time, Jung Young was stopped in broad daylight by several gunmen. They robbed her of her pick-up truck and the money she was carrying. Thankfully they did not fire at her point-blank when she resisted. It took her a while to get over that traumatic experience.

Just as there is pain, there is also joy in the ministry. Jung Young introduced me to a shy and modest twenty-year-old Khmer lady. Her name is Sokha. She was helping at the centre working on the computer. She was brought to the centre and was taken care of by the staff for several years. She matured beautifully and was smart and responsible enough to make it to the local university. With her exposure to the ex-pat staff, she picked up the English language to a point of proficiency that was noticed by the faculty. She has since graduated and works as a translator in the university.

'She volunteers to help at the centre,' said a proud Jung Young. 'It's her way of expressing her gratitude for what God has done for her.' Just as God has made a difference in her life, she desires the same for other children.

Another problem emerging in Cambodia is children at risk. Increasingly, experts tell us, there is a need to address this problem. Children are at risk of physical, sexual and familial abuse. Often in these cases, the need is to provide a safe haven, albeit short-term (to start off with) for these children. In the long-term, the partnership between NGOs will ensure progressive care, and the involvement of the local churches will provide the integration into society. For this reason, Mercy Teams International, the holistic ministry of OM in East Asia, headed by Dave and Dawn Greenfield, is establishing a safe place to look after this group of children at risk. This project followed a successful project a year earlier where MTI (Mercy Teams International) provided building materials, together with the Red Cross, to 400 families whose homes (more like bamboo shacks) were destroyed by fire.

The encouraging sign is that churches in the region are rising to the challenge of missions nearer home, and are focusing on the holistic needs in Indo-China, much like they are putting people and resources into Cambodia in the hope that for many, life will become more bearable, and eternally more meaningful in the Person of Jesus Christ.

# Chapter Seventeen

# Travel perks, travel quirks

Don't travel hard; travel smart.

This chapter about travel perks and quirks is an easy one to write. It is the fun part as well. However, let me assure you that most trips I have taken and continue to take are uneventful, and are quite predictable. It is not as if I meet drama each time. Except perhaps on the one occasion when I was waiting for a flight out of the Singapore Changi Airport around midnight. I noticed several security personnel clustered together and out of curiosity, I went nearer to find out what had caused the commotion. To my amazement, it was Her Majesty, Queen Elizabeth, the Queen of England, browsing at the Duty Free shop, a mere five metres away. I had never seen her close up – I suppose most people don't either. She looked beautiful in person – I was mesmerised. Then to my amusement I recognised one of the persons accompanying her. She was none other than the board member of OM Singapore, assigned by the Foreign Affairs office to accompany the Queen on her one-hour transit. I was tempted to pass on to Her Majesty my condolences for the death of her sister and mother in the same year, but that was wishful thinking, of course.

Let me share with you some memorable incidents and trips.


## First Class surpise

It finally happened to me. I travelled on First Class on an Economy ticket!

After years of air travel, I finally plucked up enough courage to ask for a seat upgrade. I believe that if you don't ask, you don't get. Most times the response I get is a polite turn-down. Chances are slim, but ask anyway! And so I did at London Heathrow.

'Is the flight full?' I asked the check-in ground staff. She said yes. 'Are you planning to upgrade anyone?' I tried. 'Afraid not,' she smiled, 'maybe next time.' 'This is my next time,' I responded in jest. Good try, anyway, I thought. After immigration, I proceeded to the executive lounge – one enjoys this perk of being a frequent flyer of the same or partner airlines. After some refreshment, I tried a different tack at lounge reception. 'I am aware the flight is full,' I started up with the receptionist, 'but I wonder if you could tell me if there is an empty row I could stretch out on?' She said as a matter of fact, there was – row 73. 'Could you block it out for me then?' She said sorry, that she couldn't as the computer system for that flight was already closed. Try the gate, she suggested.

At the gate, I repeated the same line. The attendant also apologised but encouraged me to check with the In-flight Supervisor about row 73 upon boarding the plane. So I waited until I was the last to board. As I approached the place, lo and behold, I recognised the In-flight Supervisor. 'Hello Rob!' I greeted him. Rob remembered complimenting me about the nice shirt I had worn and I had commended him for the professional manner in which he discharged his duty on a flight a year ago. After that, I wrote to Qantas commending his excellent service. Rob told me he received a copy of that letter of commendation. 'It is not every day I get a letter like that,' said he.

'Say Rob, I am told row 73 is vacant, can you transfer me there?' I requested. He checked the passenger list. He told me he would have liked to put me in Business Class but it was already chock-a-block. But he did usher me to row 73, and seated me next to a row of three empty seats – a luxury in a packed cabin. The plane took off and after dinner, dog-tired, I curled up and fell asleep.

'Hey Rodney,' I heard a voice calling me in my slumber. I opened my eyes to see Rob squatting in the aisle next to me. 'Would you like to stretch out in First Class?' Is the Pope Catholic? 'Sure,' I said, trying not to sound over-eager. Taking my hand baggage, Rob led me right up to First Class. He introduced me to the cabin crew attending the first class passengers – there were only seven of us out of the fourteen seats. As Rob sat me down, he said to me, 'This is in appreciation for what you did.'

Now that I was seated in First Class, I could not sleep! How could I? I was busy thanking the Lord and savouring the moment. The attendant gave me a personal entertainment programme with a menu of the top fifty movies of all time. I looked at my watch and saw to my dismay that I had only eleven hours left on the flight to enjoy the service. Even the toilets, with all kinds of toiletries and amenities, were luxurious. I could not resist fiddling with the half dozen or so control buttons for the seat. Eventually I settled for the flat bed – yes, a sleeping berth in the sky. The blanket was of smooth silk.

All good things must come to an end, but not before breakfast was served. The cabin crew laid a fresh piece of cloth on top of the individual table before me. Silverware came next. I could choose either freshly brewed tea or coffee. Then I had the difficult chore of choosing the bread that I liked – rolls, toast, high fibre, croissant or plain. Jams were next. There was a basket to choose from. Finally the main course – grilled sausages, bacon, ham, scrambled eggs, fried or boiled. Wow. What a treat!

When the plane touched down at Changi Airport, I was jolted back to reality. Why did it have to end so quickly, I thought. On my way out, I thanked Rob and left my business card with him. 'Next time you stop over,' I said, 'please give me a call and it will be my pleasure to take you to a nice Chinese restaurant.'

Well, what's the moral of the story? Friends would volunteer 'write nice letters!' after they heard my account. Hey, when I wrote that letter to Qantas, I didn't think I would meet Rob again. I did what I thought was a nice thing to do – showing genuine appreciation. Yeah, yeah, sure . . . so said my friends.

## Pekan Baru Express

*Been There, Done That* was the title of my first book. Having been there and done that, what was there left to surprise a seasoned traveller like me? Plenty. One trip showed me up to be quite dumb. And I suffered a terribly bruised ego.

Pete (not his real name) is a friend and colleague working in Indonesia as an English language teacher. For some time, I had wanted to pay him a visit to learn about his work and to encourage him. Pete gave me instructions on how to get to Pekan Baru – 'catch a ferry to Batam and then get the connection to Pekan Baru.'

Getting there would be a piece of cake. After booking the ferry ticket to Batam, I thought it would only be a matter of course that I would get to my destination, spend a night there with Pete, and be back the next day.

Upon arrival in Batam, I proceeded to the domestic ferry terminal. There was no lack of touts selling tickets to Pekan Baru. No problem, I would get an immediate connection. 'The daily ferry to Pekan Baru left an hour ago,' informed the ticket vendor, 'and the next is tomorrow.' Why tomorrow? I thought Pekan Baru was on the next island? To my horror, I found out Pekan Baru is right in the heart of Sumatra and the ferry would take ten hours to get there! I felt like a full-blown idiot.

Now that I had one day to kill with nowhere to go, I started figuring out how to spend the day and night. I remembered a couple who had moved from Jakarta to Batam some years ago. A few phone calls later, I was on my way to stay with Rex and Ina.

Next morning, I joined about one hundred or more mainly Indonesian passengers for the trip to Pekan Baru. Everyone seemed to avoid the first row at the bow. I settled into it and was alone much of the trip.

As the ferry plodded on, I noticed we were stopping at every island to pick up and drop off passengers. No one told me it was an island hopper. Lunch was pro-vided free of charge. The boatman, only nineteen years of age, struck up a conversation with me. He wanted to practise his limited English. For that, I was offered an extra packet of lunch. He pointed to me another mistake I had made – I had paid for a ticket that was good only up to the last drop off point (where passengers could catch a bus to Pekan Baru but no one told me!). I forked out extra ruppiahs to pay the shortfall. This boatman offered to take me to the First Class section on the upper deck, but by then I was happily settled into my bow seat. I managed to finish a book and listen to the Bible on CDs (all the minor prophets!). That was time well redeemed. Dusk had already settled when the ferry pulled into Pekan Baru. Pete was standing on the jetty waiting for me.

For the next two days, Pete showed me around the town and its outskirts on his motorbike, and alerted me to the spiritual needs. We visited the language centre where he teaches and I met with some of the directors. Then he took me to his bachelor's pad in a village crowded with people he was seeking to reach. Pete's room was bare and simple. But he was contented. I was impressed by his commitment and his sacrificial service. Pete decided to take me to visit his brick-maker friend – a 15 kms bike-ride away. It was a bumpy and dusty ride. We spent an hour watching his friend and family make bricks. Then we sat down for a cup of tea and talked. It would be some time before the gospel was mentioned. We left cordially just as we were received cordially.

By the time we got back to town, we were both coated with a film of soot from the firewood used for cooking dinner in every home. That night, Pete took me for one of the best meals I have eaten in my entire life. The region near Padang is renowned for Padang (meaning field) food.

The following day, I decided to catch the shuttle flight back to Batam. From there I took the ferry back to Singapore. What was supposed to be a day trip took me four days. If there was one thing I have learned, it would be to listen more and presume less!

### Jerry, my Indonesian *tikus*

I was a regular at this one-star hotel in Jakarta North. I stayed there for convenience as it was near our office, but mainly because it was cheap. It even boasted a pool. Its name, translated into English, is 'Hotel Beautiful'. I still do not know why it is called beautiful when it is located next to what looks like a swamp. Anyway, there I was over-nighting on my fourth stay at 'Hotel Beautiful'.

Alone in my room, I was preparing to sleep. As I read my Bible, I noticed it in the corner of my eye – something black was zigzagging across the room. I went after it to find out what it was. To my chagrin, it was a 6-inch long hotel mouse. It disappeared into a corner and I left it at that. I checked the walls but could not find any hole so I concluded it must have left the room.

In the middle of the night I heard something like a hotel brochure fall off my bedside table. I smiled and thought to myself 'must be Jerry'. I hoped it would not bother me by nibbling at my ear. It didn't.

Early in the morning, I got up to go to the toilet. The curtains were drawn and the room was still dark. As I was relieving myself I happened to look down into the toilet bowl. With eyes still unfocused, I saw something black moving in the water. I reached out for the switch to turn the light on. To my surprise it was my roommate Jerry. It survived the flood and sat there in the shallow water. I dropped the toilet seat to keep it from jumping out – not that it could. I had an idea – Rasdin, our Indonesian staff, was coming to pick me up shortly. I would play a prank on Rasdin.

As soon as Rasdin entered my room, I insisted that he use the toilet. When he flipped the seat up, he cried out, '*tikus!*' – Indonesian for mouse. We had a good laugh. We decided to let housekeeping find out for themselves.

At the reception, the staff was extremely apologetic and embarrassed about the tikus. I assured her that I didn't mind the hotel pet at all. The OM staff vowed never to put me up there again. I wasn't going to argue.

## The Art of Hospitality

The Bible encourages us to practise hospitality – 1 Peter 4:9. For all you know, like Abraham, you may have 'entertained angels without knowing it' – Hebrews 13:2. Having experienced hospitality, the least I can do is to reciprocate the gesture. One time I treated a complete stranger to a meal after hearing the long distance he had travelled. If you do get the chance I hope you will practise the gift of hospitality.

I was tired having arrived at the Inchon International Airport outside Seoul, Korea. Su Yong, the director of OM, took three hours in heavy traffic to collect me. By the time we had our dinner and reached the hostel I was going to stay at, it was already 11 at night. Unlike winter when rooms are sufficiently heated, rooms in the summer have inadequate ventilation. I had stayed here several times before and there was no reason to complain. But as the night drew on, I was furiously attacked by mosquitoes. I covered myself with the bed sheet but it only got me sweating. Eventually I got up in search of some mosquito spray. None was found on the entire floor. When I got back to the room, I decided to hunt for the mosquitoes. I managed to kill three fat ones, heavily laden with my own blood. Next morning, I killed two more. If someone tells you not to be bothered by little things, this person doesn't know anything about sharing a room with mosquitoes!

Anyway, I was quite prepared to return to the same room the second night. The day had been long, with intensive discussions in between. After my meeting with the OM Korea Board chairman, Reverend John Oak, he asked where I was staying. He said that he knew what the place was like. After a moment's thought, he said he would like to put me up in a hotel so that I could get to relax a little. He appreciated the budget missionaries operated on and he just wanted me to enjoy this treat.

So for the remaining two nights of my last visit to Seoul, I was at the Ritz Carlton! Revd Oak insisted that I eat well and relax well. I did not tell him but I almost wept with delight at this nice gesture. I had learned to abase on the first night and it was no difficulty to abound in the remaining days! I so appreciated his gift of hospitality. Then I recalled just the month before, I had insisted that a Swiss family stay at a hotel at our expense. I wanted to bless them because they had served in Papua New Guinea for twenty or so years. I wanted to honour God's servant this way. Should I be surprised when God honours us sometimes with good and pleasant things?

## Swimming with dolphins

Sometimes in life it is good to try something out of the ordinary.

But then, what's so extraordinary about swimming with dolphins? You see kids touching and stroking them on TV. They are docile and friendly. Little did we anticipate the shock we were going to get.

My family was planning a visit to New Zealand when Morris and Sonia Wong, our would-be hosts, phoned (we always get a kick out of winging the wong number!) to ask if we would like to swim with dolphins. Without hesitation, we replied in the affirmative. As we got nearer to Kaikoura, a coastal town located on the east coast of NZ's South Island, we got nervous. We would be swimming with wild dolphins out in the Pacific Ocean! Our apprehension got the better of us as we looked at the distant snow capped mountains. As a matter of fact, we had just driven from the Fox Glacier. The ocean would be freezing. But we were not ready to chicken out – not the Hui family.

In Kaikoura, the adventure outfit organising the trip gave the twenty or so participants a briefing. Like my family, the rest were all happily chattering and smiling away. Nervously. We were then kitted up with snorkel, mask and a diving suit each. We were instructed on how to attract the dolphins – make lots of noise, splash as loudly as you could and if you got lucky they might just come and play with you. So off we went.

Half an hour later, and several nautical miles from the coast, the leader signalled the sighting of a school of dusky dolphins coming our way. At his whistle, we found ourselves in the freezing ocean. The ice-old water came as a shock but only momentarily. We remembered the instructions and started splashing frantically to attract the dolphins. Missed them. They swam away. Several minutes later, another whistle was heard, this time, summoning us back to the boat. Once back on board, the boat gave chase, or would sight another school. We didn't have long to wait. Within a short distance, we were back in the ocean. This time we knew the score and so concentrated on attracting the dolphins. I was holding the hand of my daughter Marianne when we saw something big and greyish zip past between us. It was exhilarating. Another swimmer started spinning round and round – another way to attract the dolphins, and he got lucky, one came by and swam around him several times. He was the most delighted among us.

It went on for an hour or so. By then, we were becoming accustomed to this sport. Our body temperatures were also dropping. We were told to host the heated water into our diving suits to keep warm. It worked.

It was truly a good experience and I recommend it if you have not done it before.

Later, we joined another group whale-watching. Apparently, along the coast off Kaikoura is a sudden drop in the ocean where the wall is rich with plankton and food for dolphins, whales and the occasional shark. As the boat was looking out for the whale, we came across a fishing trawler, hauling in something big. As we drew closer, we saw it was a battered 4-metre shark. It looked humongous from where we were standing.

Then it dawned on us that we had jumped into the ocean around the same spot the shark was caught. Scary!

## Caribbean reggae

At last, at forty-eight, I found my music roots in, of all places, the Caribbean.

I grew up on a diet of pop music in the sixties and seventies. At ten years of age, I could figure out and play some basic beats on the drum set. Problem was, music was never a priority in a Chinese family, and even less so in one with eight kids whose single-parent mother was barely getting by financially. An education in music would not make a living, anyway – or so the popular sentiment went. Music almost died even before it had a chance to take root in my life. I believe it was only my interest that kept the music flame from being snuffed out completely.

Why I was not born an African-Caribbean I may have to ask the Lord. Listening to their music, I thought I would fit into their culture nicely.

I was invited to pay a pastoral visit to the OM ship Logos II. It didn't take much persuasion to get me to visit especially when the ship was going to be in the Caribbean. I had never been there before and it was one trip I didn't want to miss.

St Kitts and Nevis were the two islands the ship called at during my one-week visit. I heard about Bob Marley but didn't realise he was *the* reggae supremo. From the stopover in Antigua to the two islands, I heard nothing but reggae music blaring out on the air waves, on the plane, on public systems, on TV, in shops, on buses, in passenger vans, on portable stereos, everywhere. The reggae I heard in that one week was more than I had heard in my entire life! The main instruments seemed to be the bass guitar and drums. Boom . . . boom . . . boom . . . on it went. Even when I got to sleep the beat was still booming in my head!

I knew I had to join the Caribbean Christians in one of their worship sessions to experience their kind of music. The opportunity came at one of the conferences on board where a group of Christian musicians were leading in worship. The keyboardist played like a wizard, without using any music score, like the rest of the musicians. The worship leader was a Caribbean lady. It was a delight to watch the two hundred or so Caribbean believers singing and moving together. It was a popular chorus I recognised but you had to be there to appreciate the way their bodies moved with the beat. It really made us Chinese look stiff and boring! Old and young, men and women, were all swaying in rhythmic unison. Soon I was beginning to move in rhythm with them. But I was still too self-conscious standing next to some non-Caribbean ship members.Then they started clapping, and I noticed everyone clapped on beat – most churches I have been to around the world clap off beat. Finally, I said to myself, I was with the right crowd!

Towards the end of one chorus, I was anticipating that the leader would repeat the last line twice before ending it. After all, every worship leader worth their salt should know that such a standard ending gives a heightened sense of worship. Well, this lady didn't stop at the second repeat of the last line. She kept going; five times, and then ten times. Everyone kept on singing with her. They stopped after singing the last line twenty-five times! No one was complaining. It was just too good to have to stop!

Perhaps the Caribbean saints should lead the singing and worship in heaven. I would really like that!


## *Onsen* – Japanese Bath

In my first book, I recounted my first Turkish bath experience. Twenty-six years later, I discovered the pleasure of the Japanese bath.

Nobuya Sakai, my Japanese colleague and Emer, his wife from the Philippines, introduced me to the one near the OM office in Kanazawa. I had never been to one and was curious enough to want to experience a Japanese bath. My visit being in winter was the ideal time for such an initiation.

*Onsens* are as common as the nearby local supermarkets. They are part of Japanese life and Japanese culture. The entrance fee can be anything from US$4. One can bathe as long as one wants. A one-and-a-half hour visit is just about right. So, armed with towels, shampoo and soap, Nob and I entered a fairly large *onsen* located on a hillside. The first room was the locker room, where everyone was supposed to strip naked. Having done the same as all the Japanese bathers, we entered the shower section. Showers are usually taken seated on a stool. In this onsen, there were several rows of hand-held showers. Nob had brought a small basket containing everything we needed. As a courtesy and consideration to others, bathers need to shower clean before entering the pools. Having thoroughly scrubbed and cleaned, we stepped into the 'moderately hot' pool. People from the tropics do not normally know how hot moderately hot is by Japanese standards. It was hot!

Give yourself several minutes to get accustomed to the water. Allow yourself to sink until the water comes up to your neck. Most pools are shallow enough for a bather to squat. As we settled in, with a small towel placed on top of our heads, Nob began to give me a lesson in the unspoken custom of maintaining hygiene and common courtesy. First was the shower. Second, no spitting. Third, maintain silence, or if you have to speak, speak softly. Fourth, carry a small towel for your ablution. Fifth, no running, splashing or sudden movement.

I began to notice that little was heard or said. Conversation was kept to a minimum. So was movement. Bathers seemed to be absorbed in contemplation, or they were simply relaxing or de-stressing. I found myself relaxing under these conditions. I observed too that there was some degree of modesty with the small towel despite the nakedness. Bathers were civil, polite and considerate.

After ten minutes in the 'moderately hot' pool, my body temperature was up by several degrees. I was ready for the 'extreme' pool. In this pool, the water was brownish black. Nob said it contained minerals that had some therapeutic qualities. As I lowered myself slowly into the pool, I could feel the extreme heat. It was so hot it was scathing! Yet, the old Japanese bather next to me appeared as though he was in his element. Within a minute, I was out of this madness. I felt cooked.

My next dip was the 'ice-cold' pool. What a contrast! After a few minutes, the skin at my finger tips and toe tips began to wrinkle. My body temperature began to drop again. At this point, it seemed to me the most comfortable pool would be the 'moderately hot' one. Instead, Nob, suggested the hot pool outdoors. I had never bathed in the open in winter before. We stepped out into the 3C cold wintry night air, into the small garden facing the hillside. With the small hot towel on my head, and my body immersed in the hot spring, I thought I was in third heaven! It really was refreshing, invigorating and rejuvenating – all for US$4. Not a bad deal I thought. The Japanese have got it just right!

Saunas are also found in most *onsens*, as are jacuzzis.

More than an hour later, satisfied that I was thoroughly cleansed no less than three times, we towelled dry in the locker room. Then to my horror, in walked a female *onsen* cleaning staff member (and she was not even old!), right in the middle of a roomful of stark naked and semi-naked men.

'It's all right,' Nob assured me. Another unspoken custom? This was the part I found the most amusing. Having been back several times to different *onsens*, I have yet to get used to this last unspoken custom!

## Hello Vietnam

The MV Logos' first and last visit to Saigon, now Ho Chi Minh City, was towards the end of 1974. A short six months later, Saigon fell.

In early 2001, the MV Doulos made a historical first visit to modern day Vietnam. The visit had taken several years to prepare. Peter Conlan and George Barathan, veteran ship advance personnel, spearheaded the visit. I had the privilege of being a part of this visit.

As the ship sailed up the Mekong River, youth from the communist party were at the quayside with streamers and balloons. Young Vietnamese ladies were simply gorgeous in their national outfit. The ship was in for a rousing welcome at the start of a memorable one-week visit.

After some uncertainties with permissions, we were finally able to off-load a container of essential stuff for children and a donation of books to some institutions. Several key receptions were hosted for dignitaries, ambassadors and embassy personnel, for the medical and institutional fraternities and representatives from the business community. It was a joy to see a number of pastors and Christian leaders as part of the latter group. For them, to see the ship in port and to be on board was a special experience. Several of them were young volunteers serving on board the Logos back in 1974! They have all gone through much persecution. Yet, the church is growing in HCM City.

I met an expatriate who had been in Vietnam during the war and continued his ministry of encouragement from the outside after the war. He told us about the first organised tour group that he was a part of that was allowed to visit Vietnam under communist rule. Of the 12 tourists, he was the only missionary; the rest were there on espionage! He told us how on that trip he made contact with Christian leaders – it was clandestine, in darkness and secrecy. It sounded as full of suspense as a paperback thriller. The group of leaders pleaded with him to remember them to the church outside. And that became his driving mission from that point. Today, I am told that no less than 240 ministries are involved in Vietnam.

Since then, the country has opened up. Being part of ASEAN (Association of South East Asia Nations) necessitates greater openness. But it does not mean there is complete freedom of worship. Churches are still monitored. The Doulos crew and staff were official guests of a selection of churches sanctioned by the authorities. The interaction brought great encouragement both ways. The ship's crew was able to present two International concerts at the famous downtown opera theatre, in partnership with the Communist Youth party. Just the opportunity to conduct this public event brought great delight to the local and ex-pat believers.

As a tourist, I was not subjected to the restrictions that the ship was slapped with. On the Sunday, I went with Peter to a local Baptist church for their service.

As we arrived by taxi at the church which was located next to a busy crossroads, we saw several rows of chairs lined on the public walkway outside the main entrance. At least fifty worshippers were sitting outside because the church had run out of space inside. Inside, we passed a room with another hundred or so worshippers following the service through close-circuit TV. We were immediately spotted and identified as visitors and were led directly into the sanctuary located on the second floor. Visitors' privilege, I guessed. There were at least two hundred and fifty packed like sardines into a room meant for 150. Rows of pews were arranged with little leg room in between. There was no empty gap between worshippers. It was not meant for comfort, and hey, who cared. It was a joy to be worshipping with Vietnamese Christians.

The pastor spoke in Vietnamese. Without translation, I was at a loss. I made my way downstairs and out onto the street to see what it was like. The public did not seem to mind about the worshippers seated outside on the pavement. The loud speaker was clearly audible not only for the church members – I suspected it was meant for the public as well. As the service ended, the extension room was quickly converted into a Sunday clinic and dispensary. A doctor and a couple of nurses were treating church members who had ailments.

We met the pastor. He had spent a number of years in prison for his leadership and faith. In all the 27 years the ship ministry had been absent from Vietnam, the Lord had been working in his church, as was apparent in the life of this, and many other pastors.

## Return visit to Yangon

After her first successful visit to Yangon in 1998, the Doulos returned for her second visit in January 2002.

The difference between the first and the second visits was obvious. As the authorities were now familiar with us, it was less tense. The security and customs were quite relaxed – ship members were not searched every time they disembarked or embarked like before. The biggest difference was that the public were allowed to visit the ship, and to purchase books. This was an incredible answer to prayer when we realised that the import of foreign literature had been illegal for the past four decades. Opportunities abounded with relative freedom for the ship members in churches, institutions, at receptions, functions and orphanages. Church leaders again packed the lounge twice to attend a Christian Leaders' Seminar. The highlight was the meeting held on board for two hundred or so Buddhist monks. What an unusual sight to see men in saffron robes packing the main lounge. A New Testament was given to each one of them at the end of the meeting and some were disappointed when we ran out!

It was a great encouragement to me to see our work grow. We now have several Burmese serving on OM and are looking forward to more getting involved in missions in the future.

# Chapter Eighteen

# In the long run

Run in such a way as to get the prize.

(1 Cor. 9:24, NIV)

I love running.

I started running about thirty years ago. I have maintained this cheap – only a pair of running shoes, T-shirt and shorts are needed – form of exercise through the years. Of late, I have been running with a passion.

Running on the relatively flat terrain in Singapore is easy. It's just the monotonous flatness and the heat that make running a challenge. There's always some anticipation whenever I am travelling – the new location, a change in terrain and landscape, the cooler climate and in some situations, different tread-mills (for indoor-running) – add variety to this regimen.

Why do I love running? Although the initial part of a run can be heavy going due to stiffness and the heat, once I get into the rhythm, it becomes pleasurable. But the feeling is best felt at the end of each run when I reach my goal. Doctors say exercise, physical assertion and perspiration are good for health. I can't agree more. I have been resting well and have never felt fitter. With the number of trips I take overseas, I believe maintaining physical fitness has made me less prone to physical ailments. But this is only part of the reasons for my love of running.

If you talk to a long-distance runner, they will tell you that long-distance running has much to do with endurance. Or perseverance. Herein lies my motivation for running. Long-distance running demands so much from the body physically. The lungs are pushed to the limit on a steep climb or when one increases speed. Perspiration is invigorating but it can be risky if dehydration is not replenished with water intake. The arm muscles get tired from swinging and the elbows ache when locked at a certain angle. The worst punishment is on the legs. Imagine the pounding your heels receive on each run – only a good pair of running shoes can prevent greater impact. Never be stingy in getting a good pair of running shoes! Unfortunately, many runners, like me, suffer from knee injury after a prolonged period of running. This is part of life's wear-and-tear, aggravated by too much or careless running. This setback may well be the reason I stop running in the future. I am painfully aware of the limitations of my body as I grow older. Some things have to give!

Before I get carried away, let me bring in the balance. The Bible says 'For physical training is of some value, but godliness has value for all things, holding promise for both the present life and the life to come.' (1 Tim. 4:8, NIV)

My physical regimen only serves to add value to my spiritual training. I find in running a relevant analogy to my spiritual life. Some people train their body at the expense of their spirit. The spirit needs greater attention and training. At the end of life, the physical may give, but not the spirit.

Just as long-distance running involves endurance, the spiritual life demands no less. Alas, many Christians run as though they are in a 100 m sprint – all exuberance and energy – only to discover that the finishing tape has been moved 42 kms down the road. It is a marathon! There is no way you can sustain your stamina for 42 kms running at a sprinting pace. The heart can only take so much. There is a limit to our   energy. Small wonder that many young Christians just give up running the race. They are not mentally and spiritually prepared for the long run.

Hebrews 12:1 says, 'let us run with perseverance the race.' Regard the Christian life as running a marathon. To run a marathon, endurance, perseverance, discipline and hard training are needed. Likewise, our spiritual training will take daily discipline ('I beat my body and make it my slave' – 1 Cor. 9:27); it can be punishing ('endure hardship' – 2 Tim. 4:5); it means you have to say no to things that distract (or 'sin that so easily entangles' – Heb. 12:1) and yes to character formation ('train yourself to be godly' – 1 Tim. 4:7). (All NIV)

I have been running the Christian race for more than thirty years. I started at the age of seventeen. My race is by no means finished. I hope what is written in this book will help new and young Christians to have a good start, healthy sustainability, and God willing, a fine finish in the race God has called us to run, with missions sandwiched in the middle of all that we do.

To the older, more mature Christians: use this book as a reminder. I remember once reading that we don't need instructions as much as we need reminders.

So, let me invite you to join the race.

It will not be an aimless one. Paul is a good model to follow: 'I do not run like a man running aimlessly' – 1 Corinthians 9:26 (NIV). He continues, 'I bring it [my

body] into subjection' (1 Cor. 9:27) in order to avoid dis-
qualification. (KJV)

Just a word of caution though. Running in the
Christian race at times will be an uphill battle. While
there are some big battles to face, most battles in life are
small. Still, small battles must be fought. For if we lose
in small battles, it makes losing the bigger ones a whole
lot easier.

May you win the battle, and the prize, when you have
finished running.